Do Sheep Shrink In The Rain?

Do Sheep Shrink In The Rain?

Over 500 of the most outrageous
questions ever asked

82ASK

First published in Great Britain in 2006 by
Virgin Books Ltd
Thames Wharf Studios
Rainville Road
London
W6 9HA

A catalogue record for this book is available from the British Library.

ISBN 0 7535 1179 7
978 0 7535 1179 4

The paper used in this book is a natural, recyclable product made from
wood grown in sustainable forests. The manufacturing process conforms
to the regulations of the country of origin.

Typeset by Phoenix Photosetting, Chatham, Kent
Printed and bound in Great Britain by Clays Ltd, Bungay, Suffolk

Contents

Do Sheep Shrink In The Rain?

Top Ten Questions

Q. **What is the meaning of life?**

A. *The Meaning of Life* is a 1983 Monty Python film. In Douglas Adams' *The Hitchhiker's Guide to the Galaxy*, the answer to the meaning of life/universe/everything is, inexplicably, 42!

Q. **Statistically what is the best chat-up line?**

A. According to the *Daily Express* in a recent survey of 1000 adults. Top 2 chat-up lines: 'Can I buy you a drink?' & 'You don't know me but I dreamt about you last night.'

Q. **What came first, the chicken or the egg?**

A. Dinosaurs were laying eggs millions of years before chickens evolved from the archaeopteryx. So in evolutionary terms, the egg came before the chicken!

Q. Who is the only player to have scored against every team in the Premiership?

A. Andy Cole scored against every team that has been in Premiership except Reading and Swindon. He is the second highest scorer in Premiership History.

Q. Who am I?

A. Famous Peter Parker/Spiderman quotation: 'Who am I? You sure you want to know? The story of my life is not for the faint of heart...'

Q. Will I pull tonight?

A. You are more likely to pull in a nightclub if:
1. You get and maintain eye contact with someone;
2. You are assertive but not pushy;
3. You can dance.

Q. **How old am I?**

A. According to 2004 National Statistics, the average age in the UK is 38.6 years, an increase on 1971 when it was 34.1 years. Possibly you are around this age.

Q. **Who has been sent off most times in the history of the Premiership?**

A. Patrick Vieira and Duncan Ferguson have received more red cards than any Premiership footballer: 8 each. Vieira's over 9 years, Ferguson's over 12 years.

Q. **Why are the Ashes called the Ashes?**

A. The Ashes trophy allegedly contains burnt bails from the 1882 match at the Oval when Australia beat England. They represent 'the death of English cricket'.

Q. **Why do men have nipples?**

A. The presence of nipples in male mammals is a genetic architectural by-product of nipples in females. So, why do men have nipples? Because females do.

Human Body Questions

Q. **Is human flesh white meat or red meat?**

A. White meat: pale-coloured meat; red meat:
meat that is dark in colour before cooking.
Human flesh would be red meat with
variations due to individual levels of
myglobin.

———

Q. **What is the correct pH for human blood
and urine?**

A. The normal pH of human arterial blood is
approximately 7.40 (normal range is
7.35–7.45). The pH of urine ranges from 4.5
to 8.

———

Q. **Can a human live without their spleen?**

A. Humans can live without a spleen but would
be predisposed to a wide range of infections.
Vaccinations and antibiotics can counter
this though.

Q. **Where does all the snot come from?**

A. Snot, mucus or phlegm is a sticky or slippery secretion of the lining of various membranes of the body; inorganic salts, saliva and mucin (protein).

Q. **What is lichen sclerosus?**

A. Lichen sclerosus et atrophicus (LSA) is an inflammatory skin disease, usually on the genital area. Typical lesion are white papules on vulva & perineal region.

Q. **Can you drown through your bum?**

A. Since the rectum is not connected to the lungs you will be pleased to know it is not possible to drown through your bum.

Q. **Can you have a breast enlargement done on the NHS?**

A. It is possible to have breast implants on the NHS, but it is not easy & it can take a long time. Key issue is whether problem is affecting your mental health.

———

Q. **Can anxiety be treated with herbal pills?**

A. Kava (*Piper methysticum*) is a herb that is used widely in Europe for nervous anxiety, tension, agitation and insomnia. St John's wort most common.

———

Q. **Can you cry underwater?**

A. Yes, you can cry underwater, just like you can pee & sweat underwater. But you can't sneeze! 3 types of tears: for cleaning eyes, reflex and weeping.

Q. Can men get thrush?

A. Men do get thrush due to yeast infection. Candida can cause itching, redness & soreness of glans & foreskin; some men's foreskins swell & become cracked.

Q. At what period in history did women start shaving their body hair?

A. Research by Christine Hope says businesses 'encouraged' American women to shave their underarms around 1915, when sleeveless fashions became popular.

Q. Why is belly button fluff always blue?

A. Belly button fluff is often blue due to common blue tint in clothing, along with a combination of fibres, dead skin cells and body hair.

Q. If another person's hair lands on you, is it possible for it 2 root into your skin and randomly be there?

A. No – hair is not a living cell. It 'grows' because it is continually produced in the hair follicles in skin. Otherwise a very easy cure for baldness!

Q. How many pints of blood in a grown-up?

A. 9.7 imperial pints (or 5.5 litres) is the amount of blood in the body of an average adult. You could save 3 lives by donating one pint of blood.

Q. How far does a human intestine stretch if pulled in a straight line?

A. The intestine is the alimentary canal extending from stomach to anus. Human intestine is 6 to 7 metres long (20–28 feet).

Q. **If you were born blind do you dream in pictures or in sound alone?**

A. Expert Cecil Adams: 'Dreams of the congenitally blind contain no visual elements & consist predominantly of sound plus smell, touch & sense of movement.'

Q. **Why can't we tickle ourselves?**

A. When a movement is self-produced, its sensory consequences can be accurately predicted, and this prediction can be used to remove sensory effects.

Q.   If you dream of a stranger is it a creation of your subconscious or is it someone you have already met?

A.   Strangers in dreams are mainly displaced persons that are drawn from the list of persons you know by face and name. May be idealised or demonised lover.

———

Q.   How do you spot a liar?

A.   When lying, the eyes shift down to either the left or right. Hands over mouth, touching nose or ears, or fingers moving and tapping are other signs.

———

Q.   For how long can the average human male aged 20–30 years survive on beer alone?

A.   Most people can survive for weeks (50–80 days) without food but only days (3–14) without water. Alcohol dehydrates the body, so suggest less than this.

Q. Is it true that if you lick certain amphibians, i.e. frogs, then you start tripping out?

A. Toads from the genus *Bufo* produce a toxin from their parotid glands, bufotenine, which has hallucinogenic properties. Licking this would cause a 'trip'.

———

Q. How long is the world's longest fart?

A. The farting world record belongs to Bernard Clemmens of London, who managed to sustain a fart for an officially recorded time of 2 minutes 42 seconds.

———

Q. Why do I fart after I ejaculate?

A. You must have a 'high-amplitude propagating contraction' at ejaculation, from top of large intestine to just above rectum, which pushes gas out as flatulence.

———

Q.   **Why is poo brown?**

A.   Your poo is brown due to bile that is excreted by the gall bladder at the beginning of the small intestine to aid fat digestion.

———

Q.   **What would happen if I ate my own poo?**

A.   Coprophagia: consuming one's own faeces involves risk, as the bowel bacteria and eggs of parasitic worms are not safe to ingest. You could get very ill!

———

Q.   **Why does poo not flush away every time?**

A.   It's the healthy poos that actually float! If a poo does not flush, it is likely to be because either it's a healthy poo or it's too large to go down!

Q. If I were to crap my pants, how long would it take for my arsehole to become sore?

A. It's recommended that you get out of the drawers as soon as possible. It could take as little as 10 minutes for a rash to appear.

Animal
Questions

Q. What is the llama population of Australia?

A. In Australia there are about 68,000 alpacas and 1,000 llamas. Did you know Bolivia has 3 million llamas? It's the largest llama population in the world!

———

Q. Do llamas have cloven hooves?

A. The llama has cloven hooves, and so does the cama, the camel-llama hybrid. Spanish conquistadors first encountered the llama in 1528.

———

Q. What's a baby llama called?

A. A baby llama is known as a cria (Spanish for baby). They weigh around 25 pounds when new born and are nursed by the mother for 4–6 months.

Q. **What type of slug hangs from a tree to have sex?**

A. Leopard slugs have sex by intertwining their bodies then hanging from a branch suspended by mucus slime. Slugs are hermaphrodites so both will lay eggs.

———

Q. **What colour is a polar bear?**

A. Polar bear hairs are completely transparent and hollow. The bears normally appear white as the hairs scatter visible light. Their skin is actually black.

———

Q. **Are slugs poor snails who can't put a roof over their head or are snails gypsy slugs?**

A. Slugs are gastropod molluscs without shells, in contrast to snails. The loss of the shell is a derived character of evolution. Not poor but rich!

Q. **What bird's egg is shaped so that it can't fall off cliffs?**

A. Highly conical eggs are seen in cliff-nesting birds, including puffins & gannets. The egg of the common murre wobbles in a circle rather than rolling.

———

Q. **Do sharks lay eggs or carry their young?**

A. Most sharks pups hatch from eggs inside the Mother's oviduct and are born alive. Some sharks lay eggs on the sea floor, others develop in the placenta as with mammals.

———

Q. **Does the bear shit in the woods?**

A. Bears live in a variety of habitats, from the tropics to the Arctic to forests to snowfields. Wood-dwelling bears definitely defecate in the woods!

Q. How do whales sleep without drowning?

A. Two basic methods of sleeping: resting quietly in the water, vertically or horizontally, or sleeping while swimming slowly next to another animal.

Q. How do whales sleep without sinking?

A. Whales have to think about breathing. If they fell asleep for hours, they would die. They let one half of the brain sleep so they are semi-conscious and can wake themselves up if necessary.

Q. If jellyfish have no brains can they feel pain?

A. Jellyfish do have a very simple type of nervous system known as a nerve net. However, as there is no brain to connect to, they have no sense of pain.

Q. What noise do badgers make?

A. According to www.badgers.org, when threatened the Eurasian badger will make 'menacing noises', possibly hissing and spitting. The hog badger makes grunting noise.

———

Q. How far can a llama spit?

A. A llama can spit accurately for 5–6 feet. They generally only spit when provoked. Usual reason is to settle an argument over food. Spit is chewed-up grass.

———

Q. Do ducks have a tongue and teeth?

A. Ducks do indeed have tongues. Recently discovered, ducks quack with regional accents. They do not have teeth, but have a gizzard, which grinds up food.

Q.   **What is a pangolin?**

A.   Pangolin: long-tailed, scale-covered
mammals of order *Pholidota*. Have long
snout & sticky tongue 4 eating ants and
termites. Also called scaly anteater.

———

Q.   **Does a bee poo and wee?**

A.   Bees eliminate waste as one, not separately
as wee and poo. Waste comes out of the gut
at the end of the tail. It's yellow, and the size
of a pinhead.

———

Q.   **Do snakes have a skeleton?**

A.   Snakes have a light skeleton, with 100–300
vertebrae connecting to ribs, and is made in
such a way so as to enable it to have free
movement.

Q. Can squirrels swim?

A. Squirrels are not afraid of getting in water, and can quite easily 'doggy paddle' their way across narrow stretches of water.

Q. If I were to stack badgers on top of each other how many would I need to equal the height of the Eiffel Tower?

A. The Eiffel Tower is 300 metres tall and the average badger 30cm. So you would have to stick 1,000 badgers on top of each other to equal the height.

Q. How many eyelids does a dog have?

A. A dog has 3 eyelids, the main upper and lower lids, and a 3rd lid hidden between them in the inner corner of the eye.

Q.   Have lions and tigers which have been cross-bred, called ligers?

A.   The liger is a cross between a male lion and a female tiger. It looks like a giant lion, with diffused tiger stripes. Like tigers, ligers like swimming.

Q.   Do fish have sex, if not how do they reproduce?

A.   Fish mate differently. The majority of fish spawn (F & M release eggs & sperm into water at same time – fertilisation). Some fish make nests (F lays eggs, M swims over releasing sperm). Some sharks exhibit internal copulation (M bites F fins to hold onto her, sperm passed to F by adapted fins called claspers).

Q. What happens if you don't milk a cow?

A. If a cow is not milked all its life, nothing happens. If it is milked regularly then stopped, its body cannot adapt easily, and it may get mastitis & even die.

Q. What animal has the biggest penis and does it have oral sex?

A. Biggest penises are found among cetaceans (inc. dolphins and whales). Penis of large Rorqual whale is 10ft long. Does not partake in oral sex.

Q. Which is cleverer, a pig or a whale?

A. Studies show pigs are smarter than dogs and even dolphins. They're easier to train too. Whales have the biggest brains known to man, but aren't smarter.

Q.   Why can't cows walk down stairs?

A.   Cows can walk up stairs, but not down them
     (if steep). This is because of the structure of
     their knee ligaments, which limits bending of
     their legs.

———

Q.   When an elephant ejaculates, how much
     is there?

A.   When an elephant ejaculates, it could
     contain 50–100mls of semen, that's roughly
     half a mug full.

———

Q.   Do worms have mouths?

A.   Worms do have mouths. Earthworms possess
     very strong mouth muscles; they do not
     have teeth. They eat fallen leaves and also
     get nutrients from the soil.

Q.   **How many animals did Moses take on the ark?**

A.   Moses took none, it was Noah who took animals on the ark. There are 4,260 species of mammals so would have been at least 8,500.

————

Q.   **Do fleas have tongues?**

A.   No, fleas have eyes and antennae that detect heat and vibration, which indicate a possible meal nearby. Fleas ingest blood of animals through a 'snout'.

————

Q.   **Is there a spider in the UK that has a bigger body than a 50 pence coin?**

A.   Largest UK spider in the wild is the raft spider, which grows up to 22mm, slightly smaller than a 50 pence coin. Its leg span is about 70mm.

Q.   **Which animal produces the largest poo?**

A.   Usually the bigger the animal the bigger the excrement – the biggest poo belongs to the bull elephant which can fill a wheelie bin!

Q.   **What animal does cashmere come from?**

A.   Cashmere: fabric made from the soft fleecy undergrowth of the Kashmir goat, from the high plateaus of Asia, such as China. Used in clothes production.

Q.   **Is it true that more people die of hippos than any other animal (not humans)?**

A.   In Africa hippos kill more people than any other animal apart from mosquito, due to their habit of overturning boats and attacking their occupants.

Q. **How many insects live on our planet?**

A. Estimated that 30 million species of insect live on earth, accounting for 95 per cent of animal species. Nobody has estimated the total number of insects.

Q. **What is the most deadly animal?**

A. According to LiveScience, the deadliest animal is the mosquito. They often carry malaria parasites, so causing deaths of more than 2 million people a year.

Q. **What is the world's heaviest animal?**

A. Blue whale is largest & heaviest animal in world (can live for 100 years). Fully grown blue whale may be 30m long, much bigger & heavier than any dinosaur!

Q. **What animal is the Walt Disney character Goofy?**

A. Goofy is a dog, albeit more of a human kind of dog than Pluto. His original name was Dippy Dawg in cartoon shorts of the 1930s.

———

Q. **What are the other 3 kingdoms after plants and animals?**

A. 5 kingdoms: Monera (bacteria), Protists (including protozoa and algae), Fungi, Plants, Animals. Some biologists recognise 6 kingdoms.

———

Q. **Did Garrincha, the famous Brazilian footballer, lose his virginity to an animal? If so which animal?**

A. Legend has it that Brazilian football hero Garrincha lost his virginity to a goat. He is known to have had at least 14 children and killed his mother-in-law!

31

Q. How many spiders do you eat during your life while sleeping?

A. It's a widely reported myth that you will swallow 8 spiders during your lifetime. In fact it's very unlikely that you'll swallow any.

———

Q. What animal licks its wrist to stay cool when it's hot?

A. Kangaroos lick their wrists and forearms when it's warm. It cools the blood in a network of tiny blood vessels near the surface of the skin.

———

Q. Is a natural sponge a coral or a land-based plant?

A. The natural sponge is the skeleton of the porifera, a sea animal. All animal matter has been removed by maceration and washing.

Q. Aside from humans, what is regarded the most intelligent animal on the planet?

A. Large monkeys/chimpanzees generally develop intellect superior to that of other mammals. They are thoughtful creatures, with excellent memory.

Q. What is a pizzle?

A. Pizzle: 1. The penis of an animal, especially a bull. 2. A whip made from a bull's penis.

Q. Is it still legal to give fish as prizes at fairs and galas, etc?

A. Though the Animal Welfare Bill was going to make it illegal to give away goldfish as fairground prizes, the govt decided to keep it legal, but only for over 16s.

Q.   **What is the fastest bird of prey?**

A.   Peregrine falcon is the fastest animal (and therefore bird of prey) on earth. Its diving speed has been accurately measured at up to 217mph (350km/h).

Q.   **Is there an animal called a Woodchuck, and does it chuck wood?**

A.   Groundhog (*Marmota monax*), aka Woodchuck, is a rodent of the family *Sciuridae*. Not known to chuck wood; name comes from Algonguian word 'wuchak'.

Q.   **What is sweetbread? Pancreas or testicles and what animal is it from?**

A.   Sweetbreads are the pancreas or thymus gland of a calf, lamb or piglet. Considered a good source of vitamins and minerals.

Q. What is the name of the animal created from a male horse and a female donkey and what is the name of one from a female horse and male donkey?

A. Breeding a male donkey to a female horse results in a mule; breeding a male horse to a female donkey produces a hinny.

Q. Does my pet rabbit feel emotion?

A. Recent research suggests that animals do experience emotion in a similar way to humans, though they lack certain cognitive insights.

Q. When copulating, is it only humans that do it face to face or does another animal?

A. Bonobo apes have sex face to face, as do whales, dolphins, dugongs, manatees, beavers and sea otters.

Q.   **What animal does a chamois cloth come from?**

A.   Chamois or shammy/chammy leather comes from an extremely agile goat antelope of mountainous regions of Europe, with upright horns & backward-hooked tips.

___

Q.   **Which was the first animal in space?**

A.   1st animals in space were the monkeys Albert 1 & 2. They died in the late 1940s in the nose cones of captured German V-2 rockets during US launch tests.

___

Q.   **What's the largest animal you can knock out with one punch?**

A.   The biggest animal knocked out by a human punch seems to be a horse. Boxer Roberto Duran claimed to have knocked out a horse to impress a girl.

Q. **Why is it so rare to see white dog poo these days?**

A. White poos are a result of a large intake of calcium. Dogs commonly have white dog poo when they eat bone marrow. Dogs eat fewer bones these days.

Q. **Does llama dung have any odour?**

A. Llama dung is pelletised and nearly odourless. It is used by Indians in the Andes for fuel. The pellets burn like charcoal but the smoke has a pungent aroma.

Q. **Why does an oyster have a pearl?**

A. Pearls begin as irritants (sand, parasite, etc.) trapped in the oyster's shell. The oyster coats the intruder with layers of nacre, a solid, slick material.

Q. **My wife has just eaten a corkscrew piece of pig. Do you think it was penis or tail?**

A. Both pig tails and penises are eaten as delicacies, especially in France. Penis is corkscrew shaped, tail is much straighter. So probably a pig penis.

———

Q. **Were chickens and cavemen on the planet at the same time ever?**

A. Cavemen were on the planet 230,000 to 29,000 years ago; red jungle fowl a direct ancestor of the chicken, appeared 5,000 years ago. So caveman & chicken didn't co-exist.

———

Q. **How tight is a perch's arse?**

A. The cloacal opening just behind the anal fin on the perch is soft and slight pressure can cause this to open – indicating not very tight at all.

Q. What sort of animal is a git?

A. There is no species called 'git' but your gastrointestinal tract, GIT, the system which extends from the mouth to the rectum, houses 400 different species.

Crime and Law Enforcement Questions

Q. Who is Ted Kaczynski?

A. Ted Kaczynski, aka the Unabomber, is an
American terrorist convicted of murder for
sending mail bombs to people for 18 years,
killing 3 & wounding 29.

Q. What was the crime that the A-Team was
supposed to have committed? ('... A crack
commando team was sent to prison by a
military court for a crime they didn't
commit...')

A. In an effort to end the Vietnam War, the
A-Team was ordered to rob the Bank of
Hanoi. When they returned to base
successful, their commanding officer was
found murdered and the base destroyed; no
proof existed that they had acted under
orders.

Q.   Why do you get hungry when you smoke weed?

A.   Italian researchers found that cannabis replicates (albeit with much greater intensity) a hunger regulation effect that the body produces naturally with endocannabinoids.

Q.   A baby was found in a cement block a few years ago in Cumbria, I think, and before they opened the block to examine the body and solve the murder they X-rayed it. How did they know the body was in there if it hadn't been opened?

A.   The police discovered a sole concrete block in a disused garage and treated it as suspicious. X-rays were performed and the body was discovered.

Q.   Why are joints so good?

A.   Joints are good as they allow limbs to flex.
     They're particularly good on bees – in fact
     they're the bees knees!

Q.   What side effects does Ecstasy have?

A.   Short-term side effects of Ecstasy include
     anxiety, paranoia, nausea, hallucinations,
     muscle cramping, blurred vision. Long-term
     effects being investigated but thought to
     include liver damage, depression and brain
     damage.

Q.   I really fancy consuming the family tabby
     cat. Is this legal and can you suggest a
     tasty recipe?

A.   It is illegal in the UK and the USA to serve
     or eat cat meat. In some Asian cultures,
     however, cat is commercially available.

Q.   How long does cocaine and Ecstasy stay in
      your system for? And if you have a health
      check for employment will it show up?

A.   Depending on intensity of use, MDMA
      (Ecstasy) and cocaine can stay in the system
      for 1–7 days. If a check-up happens within
      this period, then it will show up.

Q.   Why do people kill?

A.   Why do people kill? One motive may be
      revenge. Serial killers see it as a way of life.
      Possibly out of mercy. No excuse to kill, just
      reason and motive.

Q.   Who is Britain's most notorious killer?

A.   Fred and Rose West are two of Britain's most
      notorious serial killers. Fred hanged himself
      in Birmingham's Winson Green prison on
      New Year's Day 1995.

Q. Are there any old films that you can name that were banned at the time of release and are still banned? What was the content also, please?

A. Banned films: *Snuff* was banned in 1970s due to scenes of real killing. The 1972 Wes Craven film *The Last House on the Left* was banned in the UK until 2002, when an edited version was released.

———

Q. Which serial killer was known to have read *The Catcher in the Rye*?

A. We think you may mean David Chapman who had a copy of J D Salinger's book, *The Catcher in the Rye*, with him when he shot John Lennon.

Q. **How do magic mushrooms work?**

A. 'Magic' (Psilocybe) mushrooms contain
compounds that resemble and interfere with
normal chemicals in the body. Effects felt are
the result of disruptive, chemical
interference with the body's nervous system.

———

Q. **Is cannabis bad or good for you?**

A. Cannabis can be used as an analgesic, but
there are still risks in its recreational use
including long-term mental disorders, and
damage to immune system and lungs.

———

Q. **Which European country has the most
heroin users per person?**

A. Heroin using is most prevalent in the UK,
Italy & Portugal. Five to eight per 1,000
inhabitants (aged 15–64) use. Three to five
in France, Spain & Ireland.

Q. How many people have been electronically tagged in the UK?

A. So far around 27,000 people have been released from prison early to serve out the remainder of their sentence 'on the tag'.

Q. In law within how long after the act must a person die to be guilty of murder?

A. Murder refers to the premeditated killing of one human being by another regardless of how long before the person dies after the act is committed. Manslaughter is killing without malice aforethought.

Q. Who is Udre Udre?

A. Udre Udre (19th C) is Fiji's most notorious cannibal & tribal chief. 872 stones surrounding his tomb represent each of his unlucky victims. He ate every part of them!

Q. **Can a man beat his wife with a stick no thicker than his thumb?**

A. A myth of Old English Common Law is that a man was allowed to beat his wife with a stick no thicker than his thumb. Research has determined the phrase 'rule of thumb' to be originated by woodworkers, not legal wife-beating!

Q. **Is it an offence to dress up as a policeman?**

A. While dressing up as a police officer is not a crime, impersonating one is. There are many policeman outfits available for fancy dress.

Q. **What advantages, apart from the smaller size, does a sawn-off shotgun have over a normal shotgun?**

A. A sawn-off shotgun has about the same destructive power as a normal shotgun but it is less accurate and has less range but has a wider spread.

Q. How far away will a blank bullet kill you from?

A. Blanks contain primer & powder, but have a paper wadding as their bullet. Danger comes primarily from recoil of gun, deaths reported from contact range.

Q. If you shot a gun in the air, could the bullet kill a person when it falls from the sky if it hits you directly on the head?

A. An AK-47 fires a bullet at 780 m/s. Depending on air resistance, the bullet could go a mile up. The bullet would be fast enough (120mph) to kill on way down.

General Knowledge Questions 1

Q.   Are there different types of napalm and is it illegal under certain weapons conventions?

A.   Many types of napalm in dozens of compositions. Trade product is powder, which is mixed to form different types, e.g. Napalm-B. Use of napalm against civilian populations was banned by UN in 1980.

———

Q.   If a smoker goes into a coma for a sufficient time, do they awake without the craving they had before to smoke?

A.   Nicotine completely leaves the blood stream 8 days after the last cigarette. If in coma for longer, physical cravings would cease, but habit may remain.

Q.   Is it true that people cremated in the UK are first removed from their coffins & incinerated with other bodies?

A.   No. The Code of Cremation Practice requires that nothing be removed from the coffin – it must be placed into the cremator exactly as received.

———

Q.   In which 3 US states does one volcano lie?

A.   In the USA, Yellowstone Park is one large active supervolcano, Caldera, which has witnessed massive explosions in the past. It spans Idaho, Montana and Wyoming.

———

Q.   What is the temperature of the tip of a burning cigarette?

A.   The tip of a cigarette burns at a hot 1292° Fahrenheit (700° Celsius) when the smoker inhales. In between puffs, it burns at a cooler temperature.

Q. How does spontaneous human combustion occur and is it possible that anyone can spontaneously combust at any time?

A. Spontaneous human combustion is the burning of a person's body, allegedly without any external source of ignition. It's not a proven natural occurrence.

Q. Who invented the car cigarette lighter?

A. James Kilburg of Luxembourg devoted his life to creating the car cigarette lighter, the 1st automatic dialling phone & an automated cherry stone remover!

Q. When is the world going 2 end?

A. No one knows exactly when the world will end. The sun will cease to provide us with heat & light in 4.4 billion years, signalling the end of life.

Q.   How long is a piece of string?

A.   Wittgenstein: 'In philosophy, it is better to
     ask a question than to state an answer'; a
     piece of string will, however, always be 2x
     the length of its halves.

———

Q.   What is the funniest joke?

A.   2 hunters in wood, 1 collapses. 999 call: 'My
     friend is dead! What do I do?' Reply: 'Let's
     make sure he's dead.' A gun is heard. Guy
     says, 'OK, now what?'

———

Q.   How many Maltesers can you fit in the
     Albert Hall?

A.   Vol. of space occupied by 1 Malteser approx.
     0.12 cubic inches. Albert Hall, oval, 200ft
     length, 160ft breadth, 140ft high, cubic ft =
     3,518,584, so about 50.6bn Maltesers.

Q.   How do you like your eggs in the morning?

A.   Dean Martin doesn't mind how he gets his eggs in the morning as long he gets them 'with a kiss'. Fried is the most popular way to cook eggs for breakfast.

———

Q.   What's the stupidest thing that anyone has ever said?

A.   Stupidest thing ever said may be Brooke Shields' infamous howler: 'Smoking kills. If you're killed, you've lost a very important part of your life.' Ouch!

———

Q.   What am I thinking?

A.   'What am I thinking' is part of a Utopia song called 'I Will Wait': 'What do I know, what am I thinking, Nobody knows that the hour is getting late...'

Q. How many men can you fit in a phone box?

A. Practically, 7 people can fit in a phone box, provided they were holding each other up, etc. In terms of mass you could fit more, but not if you wanted them to live!

Q. If you fell out of a spaceship and held your breath, how long would it take to die?

A. You can hold your breath in space but likely to damage lungs. You would probably pass out/die after about 15 seconds in vacuum because of oxygen transference.

Q. Which town in England has the dirtiest birds?

A. The dirtiest birds are in London, mainly the pigeons. This is due to the smog, but even the pigeons in Trafalgar Square don't wash in the fountain.

Q. How many badgers would it take to support the Empire State Building?

A. Empire State Building is 365,000 tons. Average weight of adult Euro (not US) badger is 11kg. So, according to Newton's third law, you would need 30,102,040 badgers.

Q. If you chop up badgers, how many can you fit in a wheelie bin?

A. The average badger is 75x30x20cm. Wheelie bins are 580x710x1070cm. So you can fit 9 badgers in a bin!

Q. How much liquid would there be if you liquidised an elephant?

A. African elephants weigh up to 14,000 pounds. That is roughly 6,350 litres of mass! A whopping 1,677.6 gallons of liquidised elephant.

Q. How many spaghetti hoops can you get on the average fork?

A. 177mm long fork, with prongs of 50mm length, and each spaghetti hoop as 5mm, would fit 20 hoops. Only the outer 2 prongs could be used.

———

Q. Wendy Whopper's vital statistics?

A. Wendy Whopper's vital statistics are currently 38E–21–34; she was 80HHH–21–34 but has had a breast reduction.

———

Q. When will I die?

A. Hard to predict when somebody will die, as it can be influenced by many factors including chance. Current UK life expectancy is 81 years (female), 76 (male).

Q.   **Is it actually possible to slip on a banana skin?**

A.   A banana skin is about 80 per cent water, which is one reason why they are so slippery – so yes, it's perfectly possible to slip if you stand on one!

———

Q.   **What's the best excuse to have a week off work except a cold?**

A.   Claiming an upset stomach from eating something dodgy whilst out is a good excuse for not going to work. A sudden emergency at home is also believable.

———

Q.   **What is Easter egg in Welsh?**

A.   'Easter egg' is 'Wy pasg' in Welsh. Did you know? Vegreville, Canada is the site of the largest Easter egg in the world, it stands 31.6 feet high, and weights 5,000 pounds.

Q.   If I adopt the philosophical position of
     physicalism and an opponent levels the
     'zombie argument' against physicalism,
     how can I respond whilst still maintaining
     the physicalist position?

A.   You could counter with these:
     verificationism and the private language
     argument, behaviourism and functionalism
     or knowing and referring to qualia.

———

Q.   Is Superman a liar?

A.   Lois accused Superman of lying. He says he
     is not and tells her, 'I never lie.' In absence of
     evidence we have to believe him.

———

Q.   Name 5 things that rumble.

A.   Five things that rumble: Harley Davidson
     motorcycle, your stomach, a monster truck,
     thunder and your bum when you fart!

Q. Who is the only group with a palindrome for a name to have a hit with a song title that is also a palindrome?

A. ABBA scored a hit with 'SOS' in September of 1975. The song peaked at number 6 in the UK charts.

Q. Why are the Kaiser Chiefs so-called?

A. The band Kaiser Chiefs was named after the South African Kaizer Chiefs Football Club, the former team of long-serving former Leeds captain Lucas Radebe.

Q. How many pairs of glasses does Elton John own?

A. Over the years, Elton John has purchased over 20,000 pairs of prescription glasses, with 4,000–5,000 in his current collection.

Q. Who invented the first stacker record player so you could stack several records on top of each other? If you know what I mean?

A. Homer Capehart, as well as being a US senator, invented the jukebox (perhaps he got bored during some long-winded speeches in the senate & thought it up).

———

Q. What are the names of the members of the band Llama Farmers?

A. Band members of Llama Farmers who formed in 1997: William Brigs (guitar), Brooke Roger (drums), Bernie Simpson (vocals), Jenni Simpson (bass guitar).

———

Q. What are the names of all the bands named after Smiths' songs?

A. Pretty Girls Make Graves & Shakespeare's Sister are both named after Smiths' songs.

Sex and Sexuality Questions

Q. **Does having big feet reflect the size of a penis?**

A. In 2002, the *British Journal of Urology International* published a report that there is no relation between penis and feet, nose or hand size.

Q. **What's the most pleasurable sex position?**

A. Daily Jolt polls show that the most pleasurable sexual position for females is 'woman on top', and best for males is doggie position (second for women).

Q. **Statistically, what is the world's favourite sexual position?**

A. According to a sex survey of 6,600 people in 2004, the missionary position was most common among women (32 per cent) & 'woman on top' was most popular (37 per cent) among men.

Q.   When will I next know the love of a
     woman?

A.   National average is sex 110 times a year. So
     statistically, you are fairly likely to have sex
     within the next few days. (Obviously doesn't
     work like that in practice.)

———

Q.   How can you tell when a woman is having
     an orgasm when having sex?

A.   The simplest way is to ask her. Physical signs
     of female orgasm can include a raised pulse,
     skin flushes, pelvic spasms and shortness of
     breath.

———

Q.   What is the average length of a female
     clitoris?

A.   Entire clitoris length is from 1–4 inches,
     though only 1 inch of it is visible. The visible
     portion is called the clitorial glans and
     averages a quarter to half an inch in length.

Q. **What are the average wages for a porn actor?**

A. Porn stars are paid by the scene and get $50 to $1,500 per scene. Women tend to earn more money than men and successful actors can earn 6-figure sums.

_____

Q. **Is sperm good for your skin?**

A. Semen contains protein, which can have a tightening effect on skin. As water evaporates, protein temporarily remains, stretching out fine wrinkles.

_____

Q. **How many condoms are used every day?**

A. According to the BBC, 10 billion condoms are used every year worldwide. Means 27,397,260.3 are used every day or 27,322,404.4 in a leap year!

Q.   What is the scientific name for a bell end?

A.   The definition of bell end is the head of the
     male penis, which is called the glans.

———

Q.   Is wanking bad for you?

A.   Masturbation is fun, healthy and safe. In
     fact, it's the safest form of sex you can
     practise. So, it seems it is OK to do it
     privately in your own bed!

———

Q.   What is the average length of a female
     orgasm?

A.   Studies carried out by a researcher named
     Kinsey revealed that the average duration of
     the female orgasm is between 5–8 seconds.

Q. What size is the world's smallest penis?

A. The smallest penis recorded was 1 inch.
Smallest erect penis was 4.75 inches.
Genetics determine penis size.

———

Q. Why does pubic hair not grow like the hair on your head and when you cut it, it grows back to the same length?

A. All hair grows only in the growth phase, including hair on your head. Body hair is 'programmed' to only have a growth phase of a few months, much less than on your head.

———

Q. What is the average length of time a man can have sex before ejaculating?

A. Average man ejaculates after 7 minutes. Average woman orgasms after 40 minutes. Average number of times a man will ejaculate in his lifetime: 7,200.

Q. How do you get a girl to orgasm?

A. Most common cause of female orgasm: stimulation of the clitoris. Visible portion of this is located at the top of the labial folds.

Q. Can women ejaculate?

A. They can! The number of women who 'squirt' is unknown but estimated to be between 10 & 55 per cent. Can be urine or Skene's gland fluid.

Q. How many calories are burned after having sexual intercourse for an hour?

A. The average person can expect to burn off around 200 calories in 1 hour of vigorous sexual activity. Fewer calories burned than on a treadmill.

Q.   Why is it called a 'blowjob'?

A.   The term blowjob stems from Victorian times. Prostitutes were referred to as 'blowsy', and 'blow' was slang for ejaculation. 'Blowjob' describes the man's experience. (First recorded 1961 in the sexual sense; as recently as 1953 it meant 'a type of airplane'.

———

Q.   Why is my penis bent?

A.   Most penises are a bit bent. Peyronie's disease is a fairly rare disorder affecting the penis that can cause an abnormal angle (also presents with lumps). See your doctor if it causes discomfort.

Q. If a person undergoes gender reassignment operation, is there any chance that he/she can have it back?

A. In some cases, people who undergo gender reassignment surgery can have it reversed, but it is uncommon unless the original surgery was made without their knowledge (e.g. as a baby).

Q. What are the best foods to take into the bedroom?

A. Foods for sex play tend to be of the lickable variety like cream, ice cream and chocolate sauce. Also try ice cubes and feeding each other berries.

Q. Why do they call a lady's vagina a pussy?

A. 'Pussy' has been in use as slang for female genitalia only since the 1700s. *Bizarre* say it's because 'a girl's vagina is so eminently strokeable'.

Q. How can you tell a lady boy from a real woman in Thailand?

A. Check out the hips-to-shoulder size. Men also have a more prominent Adam's apple, but the only sure way to know is to ask or see them naked.

Geography Questions

Q. How many miles is the whole coastline of Great Britain?

A. Combined coasts of England, Wales and Northern Ireland are 3,083 miles. Scotland & its islands have 8,149 miles of coastline. Therefore, 11,232 miles in the UK.

Q. How far away in metres is the surface of the sun from the centre of the earth?

A. Distance from centre of earth to surface is 6378.137km. Distance from earth to sun approximately 149,600,000km, so total of about 149,606,378km.

Q. Is Venice sinking and how many islands are there in Venice?

A. The first Venetians took refuge on the 120 natural islands of Venice. Venice has sunk by 7cm per century for the past 1,000 years, but 24cm in the past 100 years.

Q.   When was Africa first discovered by
     Western explorers?

A.   Trade with Africa had been going on since
     Roman times and no specific person credited
     with discovery. However, the first European
     to 'rediscover' the region was Portuguese
     explorer Henry the Navigator, who set out
     to explore its West Coast in 1419.

Q.   Which continent contains the most
     countries?

A.   Africa is home to 53 countries, representing
     more than 25 per cent of countries
     worldwide. There are 47 countries on
     mainland Africa, 6 nearby island countries.

Q.   What is the world's smallest ocean?

A.   The Arctic is the smallest ocean in the
     world. It covers about 5,440,000 sq miles,
     and is Surrounded by Eurasia, North
     America and Greenland.

Q. **What is the largest by land mass continent, and the rest in order?**

A. Continents largest to smallest: Asia (44,579,000 sq km), Africa, North America, South America, Antarctica, Europe, Australia/Oceania.

———

Q. **What is the largest desert in the world?**

A. The largest desert on earth is the continent of Antarctica with 5,500,000 square miles. The Sahara desert is second largest with 3,500,000 square miles.

———

Q. **What is the biggest island in the world?**

A. World's largest island: Greenland. 2nd largest island: New Guinea. Australia (smallest continent) & Antarctica are considered continents, not islands.

Q. **How heavy are clouds?**

A. Water on earth surface evaporated by sun, condenses in atmosphere forming clouds, saturation, then release. Clouds cannot be weighed as ever changing.

Q. **If everyone in the UK stood in line how far round earth would it go?**

A. UK population is 60,441,457 (July 2005 est.). At 0.5 metres/person, you'd get 30,220,728.5 metres from starting point (which isn't all the way round)

Q. **Which sea has no coast?**

A. Sargasso Sea is a region in the North Atlantic Ocean that has no coast. It is surrounded by ocean currents and lies roughly between Cuba and the Azores.

Q. How many trees are there in the whole world?

A. The world's forest cover amounts to 3.9 billion hectares (30 per cent of the land mass). There are on average 400 trees per hectare so roughly 1,560 billion trees.

Q. What are the most densely populated countries in the world, particularly I am interested in Holland?

A. Holland is the 23rd most densely populated nation. Monaco is 1st with 23,660 per km^2. Macau and Hong Kong are 2nd and 3rd.

Q. What is the biggest village in England?

A. Many villages claim to be England's largest but the honour depends on how size is actually measured. Cranleigh is often considered the biggest, as it supports a remarkably rich and varied community life, with over 300 individual and national businesses.

Q.   Where in the modern world is the Roman
     province of Zucchabar, as featured in
     Gladiator?

A.   Zucchabar (present day Miliana, Algeria)
     was an ancient town in the Roman province
     of Mauretania Caesariensis. Wrongly
     introduced as a Roman province in
     Gladiator.

___

Q.   Where do horses originate from?

A.   Horse fossil can be dated to 54 million years
     BC. Fossils have been found in many areas
     including Scotland, France, Algeria and the
     US.

___

Q.   How many square miles is the Sahara
     desert?

A.   The Sahara desert covers 85 per cent of
     Algeria. It is the second largest desert on
     earth with 3,500,000 square miles.

Q. **Which country has the highest marriage rate?**

A. Antigua and Barbuda has the highest marriage rate with 21.0 marriages per 1,000 people (per year). The Maldives is next with 20.1 marriages per 1,000 people.

———

Q. **What country has the highest suicide rate in the world?**

A. According to a BBC report, Lithuania has the highest suicide rate for both sexes. The next highest is Russia followed by Belarus, Latvia, Estonia, Hungary and Slovenia.

———

Q. **Which 5 countries have the lowest suicide rates?**

A. The five countries with the lowest suicide rates are Sao Tome and Principe, Saint Kitts and Nevis, Jordan, Honduras and the Dominican Republic.

Q. Which countries formed the former USSR?

A. USSR: Lithuania, Georgia, Uzbekistan, Russia, Belarus, Armenia, Tajikistan, Estonia, Ukraine, Azerbaijan, Kyrgyzstan, Latvia, Moldova, Turkmenistan, Kazakhstan.

Q. What is the most polluted river in the world?

A. The Ganges River in Northern India and Bangladesh is likely the world's dirtiest river, polluted by industry, raw sewage, dead bodies and rubbish.

Q. How many countries with more than 100 million people?

A. 11 states have populations over 100 million (12 if EU counted): China, India, (EU), US, Indonesia, Brazil, Pakistan, Bangladesh, Russia, Nigeria, Japan, Mexico.

Q.   Who are the Ogboni and how can one
     join their cult?

A.   Ogboni is a fraternal institution indigenous
     to the Yoruba-speaking polities of western
     Nigeria and eastern Republic of Bénin. To
     join you have to know one.

Q.   Can you name all the countries that have
     a 'z' in their name when spelt in English?

A.   All countries that include a 'z' in English:
     Azerbiajan, Belize, Bosnia and Herzegovina,
     Brazil, Czech Republic, Kazakhstan,
     Kyrgyzstan, Mozambique, New Zealand,
     Swaziland, Switzerland, Tanzania,
     Uzbekistan, Venezuela, Zambia, Zimbabwe.

Q.   Where is the source of the Nile?

A.   Lake Victoria, Uganda, is commonly
     considered the source of the Nile but has
     feeder rivers from other lakes. Farthest
     headstream is Ruvyironza River, Burundi.

Q. **What are the ten poorest countries in the world?**

A. According to CIA, the poorest are East Timor, Somalia, Sierra Leone, Gaza Strip, Democratic Republic of Congo, Burundi, Tanzania, Malawi, Eritrea, Ethiopia.

Q. **Where is the driest place in the world?**

A. Driest place in the world is Atacama Desert in Chile. Driest inhabited place is Aswan, Egypt, 0.02 ins rainfall/year. No data on average rainfall countrywide.

Q. **What is the hottest country in the world?**

A. Djibouti is about the size of Wales, is almost totally desert and is the hottest country in the world. Antarctica and Greenland are the coldest countries.

Q. **Where is 0° longitude?**

A. 0° longitude, known as the Prime Meridian, is in the Atlantic Ocean, and extends about 380 miles south of Ghana and 670 miles west of Gabon.

Q. **What year did Persia become Iran?**

A. Persia is the Western name for the state of Iran prior to 1935. Since 600 BC, Greeks used the name Persis for Persia/Iran.

Q. **Which countries are nuclear powers?**

A. There are 7 countries with definite nuclear weapons – UK, USA, China, Russia, France, India and Pakistan. Israel, Iran and North Korea are suspected of them.

Q. **What is the deepest ocean in the world?**

A. Deepest point is in the Pacific Ocean, the Mariana Trench at 11,033 metres (36,201 feet) deep. 11"21' North and 142" 12' East, near Japan.

Q. **Which country has the highest rate of unemployment?**

A. The country with the highest unemployment rate is Liberia where 85 per cent are out of work. Kiribati and Zimbabwe are both second on 70 per cent.

Q. **What country is Timbuktu in?**

A. Timbuktu or Timbuctu is a city populated by the Songhay, Tuareg, Fulani and Moorish people in the West African country of Mali.

Q. What is the only country in the world to use every vowel in the alphabet in its name once and only once?

A. The only country in the world to use every vowel in the alphabet in its name once and only once is Mozambique.

___

Q. Where is Zealand, after which New Zealand is named?

A. New Zealand is named after Zealand in the Netherlands, birthplace of its discoverer, explorer Abel Tasman.

___

Q. Which country has most babies?

A. Niger has the highest birth rate (births/1,000 population) at 48.91, 2nd is Mali at 47.29, 3rd is Afghanistan at 47.27, 4th Chad at 46.50 and 5th Uganda at 46.31.

Q. How many countries in the world begin with the letter 'o'?

A. There is only one country in the world beginning with an 'o' – Oman, a sultanate of the SE Arabian peninsula on the Gulf of Oman, an arm of the Arabian Sea.

Q. In which country is Transylvania?

A. Transylvania consists of a region of 16 counties in central and northwest Romania. Population of 7,221,733. It means 'beyond the forest'.

Q. Where is Kangaroo Island?

A. Kangaroo Island is 112 kilometres southwest of Adelaide at the entrance of Gulf Saint Vincent. The island is 145 km long & between 900 m & 57 km wide.

Q. **What are the countries with the lowest and highest gross domestic product per year?**

A. The lowest GDPs (in USD) are Kiribati, Sao Tome & Principe (all at 62). Luxembourg is the richest country in world with GDP per capita 55,100.

———

Q. **Which country has the biggest oil reserve in the world?**

A. The most recent statistics reveal that Saudi Arabia has the greatest oil reserves, totalling 261.9 billion barrels.

———

Q. **Are there more women or men in the world?**

A. Out of the total population there are 101.3 men for every 100 women. May change if there is war. Senegal has high proportion of women: 52 per cent.

Q. Which 8 countries in the EU have red, white and blue in the flag?

A. EU countries flags with red, white & blue: France, Luxembourg, Netherlands, UK, Czech Republic, Slovakia, Slovenia & Croatia.

Q. How many camels are there in the world?

A. World population of camels is currently estimated at 20 million. Somalia is believed to have world's largest herd, with almost as many camels as humans.

Q. What did Captain Cook call Tonga?

A. Captain Cook named Tonga 'the Friendly Islands' when he arrived in the archipelago in the 1770s. The Kingdom of Tonga consists of over 170 islands.

Q. **Which country's capital city is the furthest from London?**

A. Nuku'alofa, capital of Tonga, and Wellington, capital of New Zealand, are at longitude of 175 degrees East, and are the furthest capital cities from London.

———

Q. **How many national flags feature the Union Jack?**

A. Four countries currently incorporate the Union Jack as part of their national flags: Australia, New Zealand, Tuvalu & Fiji. Of course, the UK also does so.

———

Q. **Do you know where coffee originated?**

A. Legend says a young man named Omar in Yemen near the port town of Moca first discovered coffee when he boiled some 'cherries' he found on a tree.

Q.   What are the Canary Islands named after?

A.   Islands were named Canaria (Latin *canis*, dog) because of descriptions of numerous wild dogs roaming the islands. Canary birds were named after the islands.

———

Q.   What is the capital of Uzbekistan?

A.   The capital of Uzbekistan is Tashkent, a city of approximately 2,142,700 people whose name means 'Stone City' in the Turkoman language.

———

Q.   How many grains of sand are there in the whole world?

A.   University of Hawaii tried to guess how many grains of sand are on the world's beaches. They came up with 7,500,000,000,000,000,000, or seven quintillion five quadrillion grains of sand.

Travel
Questions

Q. **What is the longest railway station name in Wales?**

A. The railway station with the longest name in Britain is Llanfairpwllgwyngyllgogery-chwyrndrobwllllantysiliogogogoch, situated in Anglesey, Wales.

Q. **What is the oldest language in Europe?**

A. Greek is the oldest recorded language of Europe. Records from clay tablets date from the second millennium BC.

Q. **Are there any trees in Iceland?**

A. There are trees in Iceland but few forests – many are rumoured to have been destroyed by the introduction of sheep! Today, Iceland plants around 4 million trees a year.

Q.   Other than Holland, in which countries is
     prostitution legal?

A.   Street-based sex work is illegal all over the
     world except for New South Wales,
     Australia, and New Zealand. Brothels/
     escorts are legal in many countries.

Q.   When was poured concrete first used in
     construction?

A.   The Assyrians and Babylonians used clay as
     cement in their concretes. The Egyptians used
     lime and gypsum cement, so poured concrete
     dates back centuries to around 3000BC!

Q.   Can you direct me to the red-light district
     from the Hotel Thorbecke in Amsterdam?

A.   De Wallen, also known as Walletjes or Rosse
     Buurt, is the largest and best-known red-
     light district in Amsterdam. South of the
     church Oude Kerk.

Q. What is the oldest language in the world?

A. The oldest language is an age-old debate. Some possibilities are: Sumerian, Akkadian, Chinese, Egyptian, Phoenician. Experts never commit to an answer.

Q. Apart from Egypt, which other countries speak Arabic as their official language?

A. Algeria, Bahrain, Iraq, Jordan, Kuwait, Lebanon, Libya, Mauritania, Morocco, Oman, Qatar, Saudi Arabia, Sudan, Syria, Tunisia & UAE all speak Arabic.

Q. Which countries don't have a taxation system?

A. There are no countries that have no taxation system. Though there are some countries that are tax havens like Dubai, Aruba, Andorra, Macau, Malta.

Q. Official English-speaking countries in Africa?

A. English is the official language in 24 African countries including Angola, Botswana, Cape Verde, Eritrea, Ethiopia, the Gambia, Ghana, Guinea-Bissau and Kenya.

Q. What are top ten beer-drinking nations per capita in the world?

A. The world's top ten beer-drinking nations are Czech Republic, Ireland, Germany, Austria, Luxembourg, Denmark, Belgium, UK, Australia, Slovakia.

Q. What is the oldest airline company?

A. KLM is world's oldest international airline still operating under its original name, established in 1919. But Chalks Ocean Airways flew from Bahamas to Florida, 1917.

Q.   **Which country has the lowest national speed limit?**

A.   Barbados & Monaco have the lowest national speed limits, of 37 mph (60 km/h).

―――

Q.   **Where is vodka from?**

A.   Vodka is believed to have originated in Poland, Belarus, Ukraine and western Russia. It also has a long tradition in Scandinavia.

―――

Q.   **What country was neutral in the Second World War?**

A.   Some of the countries that were neutral in WW2 were Sweden, Switzerland, Paraguay, Lichtenstein, Turkey, Nepal, Afghanistan, Bhutan, Spain and Portugal.

Q. **As many countries/places as u can fit in a txt that have a monarchy except UK and Thailand, please!**

A. Bhutan, Qatar, Saudi Arabia, Swaziland, Andorra, Belgium, Brunei, Cambodia, Denmark, Japan, Jordan, Kuwait, Lesotho, Liechtenstein, Luxembourg, Malaysia, Monaco, Morocco.

Q. **Where does the Sultan of Brunei live?**

A. The Sultan of Brunei lives in the Istana Nurul Iman palace, in Brunei Darussalam. Built in 1984, it is the largest private residence in the world.

Q. **What is Bulgaria famous for?**

A. Bulgaria is famous for Rose Valley, where 70 per cent of the world's rose oil is produced, and 9 UNESCO World Heritage Sites including ancient Varna Necropolis & Rila Monastery.

Q.   Why do people from Cameroon have French as their national language?

A.   Cameroon, a German colony at time of WWI, was split among the French & British as war spoils after the defeat of Germany. Language followed French settlers.

———

Q.   Has anyone ever survived a passenger jet crashing into the water?

A.   Several examples of 'successful' intentional ditchings, e.g. 23 November 1996 Ethiopian Airlines ditched near Comoros Islands – 117 of the 160 passengers were killed.

———

Q.   What is the only country outside Madagascar where you can find lemurs?

A.   Lemurs: found naturally only on island of Madagascar, & some smaller surrounding islands, including the Comoros (likely they were introduced by humans).

Q. **Do red bananas really exist?**

A. Red bananas do exist. They are grown in Costa Rica and have a creamy-white to pink flesh, with a slight raspberry-banana flavour.

Q. **If you see mountain chicken on the menu on the West island of Montserrat what would you expect to be served?**

A. Mountain chicken is one of the largest frogs in the world. It is found only on the Caribbean islands of Dominica and Montserrat. A national dish, it tastes 'like chicken'!

Q. **Where do panama hats come from?**

A. Despite name, panama hats are made in Ecuador, not Panama. Woven by hand from plant called toquilla, they came to prominence during construction of Panama Canal.

Q. How did the Sphinx in Egypt lose its nose?

A. One account of the Sphinx's missing nose states that Napoleon's artillery were responsible for this act of destruction, using the Sphinx for target practice.

Q. What are the top 10 countries with the most cases of malaria?

A. Majority of malaria deaths occur in sub-Saharan Africa: Democratic Republic of Congo, Angola, Zambia, Uganda, Congo, Gabon, Cameroon, Nigeria, Ethiopia, Chad.

Q. Who is the longest-serving president in the history of politics worldwide?

A. The world's longest-serving republican 'head of state' (actually voted for) is President Omar Bongo of Gabon (since 28 November 1967 – 39 years).

Q. How is dalasi related to the Gambia?

A. The dalasi is the currency of the Gambia. It is subdivided into 100 bututs. The dalasi was adopted in 1971 in place of the pound.

Q. Where did the food 'quiche' originate?

A. Quiche was invented in Germany, in a medieval kingdom called Lothringen (later became Lorraine, France). Quiche: from the German word *Kuchen*, meaning cake.

Q. Which country was the last to vote out its army?

A. There are 29 states that do not maintain any armed forces. Haiti was the last country to abolish defence through their own choice, doing so in 1995.

Q. **What is the biggest outdoor pool in Europe?**

A. Many places claim to have Europe's largest swimming pool. The most convincing claim is the 28-million-litre Germia Pool in Pristina, Kosovo.

———

Q. **What are the five Communist world states?**

A. China, Cuba, Laos, North Korea and Vietnam are the world's remaining Communist states. Turkmenistan is considered the sixth remaining Communist state by some.

———

Q. **Which country has the lowest age of sexual consent?**

A. Columbia, Malta and the Philippines have an age of consent of 12. The highest age of consent is in Madagascar at 21 years old.

Q.   Where in the world are the most loyal and
      disloyal partners?

A.   According to divorcemag.com, Macedonia
      has a divorce rate of just 5%, whilst Cuba
      has a 75% divorce rate and 'rampant
      cohabitation.'

Q.   Which country has the *ouguiya* as a unit
      of currency?

A.   *Ouguiya* (MRO) is the currency of
      Mauritania. It is the only circulating
      currency other than the Malagasy *ariary*.
      1 *ouguiya* being comprised of 5 *khoums*.

Q.   In which country is the world's biggest
      pyramid?

A.   The Pyramid of the Sun is the world's
      biggest pyramid. It's located half an hour out
      of Puebla near the village of Cholula in
      Mexico.

Q. In which principality in the Mediterranean, famous for its casinos, is it illegal for local residents to gamble?

A. It's not necessarily illegal for the residents of Monaco to gamble per se but they are forbidden entry to the gaming rooms of Monte Carlo.

———

Q. How much does an average camel cost to buy if I was in Morocco and what would that be in pounds?

A. According to Oxfam, a camel is worth approximately 1,505.47 MAD Morocco dirhams, 93 GBP.

———

Q. Is there a McDonald's in Myanmar?

A. Sorry, there is not a McDonald's in Myanmar (Burma). McDonald's has franchise in 119 countries. Interestingly you can get a BigMac in Antarctica but not Burma.

Q. **How many countries and which ones have 'Nkosi Sikelele' as their national anthem?**

A. 'Nkosi Sikelel' iAfrika' is the national anthem of Tanzania, Zambia and part of South Africa's anthem. It is the former anthem of Zimbabwe and Namibia.

Q. **Where can I buy an elephant?**

A. You can buy an elephant from private farms in the Kunene region (Namibia, Africa). The elephant population there has increased from 50 in 1975 to 662 in 2000!

Q. **What year did the Panama Canal first belong 2 Panama?**

A. Negotiations between Panama & the USA over the Panama Canal began in 1974. Treaties resulted in full Panamanian control effective from noon 31 December 1999.

Q. **Which civilisation is the oldest?**

A. A civilisation was flourishing in Peru over 5,000 years ago, making it the oldest known complex society. There are theories that there are older ones.

Q. **Which country has the most beautiful girls?**

A. Beauty in the eye of the beholder, a poll on www.wanderlist.com lists the Philippines and Russia as being top for most beautiful women, with India 3rd.

Q. **Who won in the Rwanda civil war, the Tutsis or the Hutus?**

A. Rwanda is best known to the outside world for the 1994 Rwandan genocide that resulted in the deaths of up to one million people. The Tutsis defeated the Hutus.

Q. **What's the best way to travel to St Helena in the South Atlantic?**

A. Fly to Ascension with RAF Brize Norton, on overnight Tri-Star (civilians allowed). Transfer from Ascension to St Helena takes 2 days on RMS *Saint Helena*.

Q. **Where is Napoleon buried?**

A. Napoleon wanted to be buried on the banks of the Seine, but was buried on Saint Helena. In 1840, his remains were taken to France & entombed in Les Invalides, Paris.

Q. **Which five countries were the first to have female prime ministers?**

A. Sri Lanka was the first with Siramavo Bandaranaike (1960), followed by Indira Gandhi of India in 1966 and Golda Meir in Israel, 1969.

Q. Are there still pirates sailing the 7 seas in this day and age?

A. In past 2 years, piracy has increased twofold. Pirates are still present in the China Sea, along the coast of Somalia, Malacca straits, coast of Columbia, etc.

Q. What language do they speak in Surinam?

A. Dutch is official language of Surinam. Surinamese also speak Sranang Tongo (which is a mix of Dutch, English, Portuguese, French and local languages).

Q. What in 1661 did Sweden become the first European country to issue?

A. First European banknotes were printed in Sweden in 1661 as temporary '*kreditivsedlar*' (credit paper). Bank of England 1st printed 'goldsmithnotes', 1694.

Q.   **Fray Bentos is in which South American country?**

A.   Fray Bentos is a town in western Uruguay, the original location of the main processing factory for the Liebig Extract of Meat Company, who make the pies.

———

Q.   **What was the cargo of the second journey of the ship the *Mayflower*?**

A.   Prior to 1609 *Mayflower*'s history is unknown. At this time it was hired to carry hats, salt, wine, hemp & vinegar to Norway, & bring home pine planks.

———

Q.   **What was the name of the first boat to go in the Panama Canal?**

A.   The Panama Canal 1st started in the 1500s, but not finished until some 400 years later. Formally opened on 15.8.1914, with the transit of cargo ship *Ancon*.

Q. How long is daylight time in Orkney on the shortest day of the year?

A. During the winter solstice in Orkney, the sun rises in the south-east at 9 a.m. and sets south-west about 6 hours later. Max. temp. less than 10°.

Q. Which country invented marshmallows?

A. Marshmallows date back to ancient Egypt. Orig. a honey-based sweet, flavoured & thickened with sap from root of Marshmallow plant (*althea officinalis*).

Fashion
Questions

Q. **Is Richard Blackwood related to Naomi Campbell in any way?**

A. Blackwood was born in Clapham, London, England. For a time he was step-brother to model Naomi Campbell (his father was married to her mother).

Q. **Which five supermodels appear in George Michael's 'Freedom' video?**

A. 5 models that appeared in the George Michael video 'Freedom' were: Christy Turlington, Tatjana Patitz, Naomi Campbell, Cindy Crawford & Linda Evangelista.

Q. **Who was Domino Harvey?**

A. Domino Harvey was the daughter of the late British actor Laurence Harvey and British model Pauline Stone. Domino dallied in fashion modelling before becoming a Los Angeles bounty hunter. She died of an apparent drug overdose in 2005.

Q. **Which supermodel said, 'I don't get out of bed for less than 10,000 dollars'?**

A. Linda Evangelista was quoted as saying 'I don't get out of bed for less than 10,000 USD a day.' She was born 10 May 1965.

Q. **What did Barbie get in the year 2000?**

A. Barbie had a very busy 2000. The fashion model range was launched & ran for president. The most significant event was the appearance of a belly button.

Q. **Can you tell me the name of the fashion model (she is not British) that I have seen in pictures who has the longest legs in the business?**

A. According to Guinness World Records, German-Brazilian model Ana Hickmann has longest legs of any female in the world. Two-thirds (117cm) of her height.

Q.   What info can you give me about Jorja
      Fox?

A.   Former fashion model, Jorja Fox has become
      a familiar face by playing major roles in *ER*,
      The West Wing and *CSI: Crime Scene
      Investigation*.

Q.   The saying 'the little black dress' is famous
      within the fashion industry. When was
      this created and why?

A.   Famous designer Coco Chanel invented 'the
      little black dress' in 1926. Previously black
      was considered a colour reserved for funerals
      and mourning. Coco Chanel has been
      quoted as saying, 'luxury must be
      comfortable otherwise it is not luxury'.

Q. What is the definition of a supermodel, how are they different to models?

A. A model is a human prop for the purpose of fashion but a supermodel is a highly paid fashion model, an elite group with celebrity status and a worldwide reputation. Supermodel is a reputed analogy to A. Warhol's 'superstars' of the 1960s and gained popularity in the 1970s.

Q. What changes in fashion occurred as a result of World War Two?

A. Main fashion changes in the UK brought by WW2 was the introduction of affordable nylon stockings by American GIs to the UK alongside denims and sneakers.

Q.   Who invented the thong?

A.   Austrian–American avant garde fashion
     designer Rudi Gernreich has been credited
     with introducing the first thong bikini in
     1974 although the style was not popularised
     until the 1980s in Brazil.

Q.   The bikini made its debut in?

A.   According to the official story, the modern
     bikini was invented by French engineer
     Louis Reard and fashion designer Jacques
     Heim in Paris in 1946.

Q.   When did it become fashionable for
     women to pierce their ears?

A.   Ear piercing is one of the oldest known
     forms of body modification. It came into
     fashion in western culture in the 1920s but
     was replaced by clip-on earrings until the
     1960s where a resurgence began again.

Q. **What is the connection between Wales and miniskirts?**

A. Miniskirt: credited to fashion designer Mary Quant, who was inspired by the Mini (car). Quant was born 11 February 1934 to Welsh parents.

Q. **When did *Vogue* magazine start?**

A. The first illustrated fashion magazine grew out of a weekly society paper that began in 1892 in New York. In between 1909–1915, American publisher Condé Nast bought the magazine and there are now 10 editions in 10 countries.

Q. **What is the name of the famous Hermes bag? And how long is the waiting list to buy it?**

A. The Hermes Birkin bag has become one of the most coveted fashion accessories ever. The Sloane Street Hermes shop: 020 7823 1014 tell us, a 1 year waiting list or you can always check for a previously owned one on eBay.

Q. **Who launched the Warehouse fashion chain?**

A. Warehouse was formed by Michael and Maurice Bennet, and Jeff Banks. The first Warehouse store opened its doors in London in 1976.

Q.   **What's the definition of a fashion victim?**

A.   A fashion victim is defined as a person who follows every clothing trend, often with no regard to whether it suits them or not (in fact, they will often look terrible as they have no taste or personal sense of style).

———

Q.   **If Paris, Rome and Madrid are centres of fashion, why do the French, Spanish and Italians dress so bad?**

A.   The dress sense may be bad in your eyes. Tastes in fashions differ from person to person. Europeans think Brits have bad taste.

———

Q.   **What funny similarities are there between babies and fashion?**

A.   Babies & fashion. Both seem fantastic, but 2 months later you find yourself wearing a vomit-coloured top and wondering where all your money has gone.

Q. I've decided I like hip hop, how can I be
more ghetto?

A. Hip-hop fashion: baggy jeans slung low,
gold/platinum chains, a fresh pair of kicks, a
bandana or doo rag tied round the head,
baseball cap on top.

Q. What's the recent craze with men wearing
pink shirts, isn't it a bit gay?

A. According to CBS Beauty & Fashion, spring
fashions for men: suits are coming back, pink
is OK for men and stripes are still hot. Pink
often seen as 'preppy' chic.

Q. What's the best time to wear a striped
sweater?

A. Striped sweaters were a fashion look for
spring/summer 2005 & perhaps should only
be worn now when you're feeling cold rather
than trying to impress.

121

Q. Why do young boys wear their jeans so low and their boxer shorts higher up? It looks awful!

A. Low jeans over boxer shorts are a prevalent fashion. Unfortunately, being fashionable and looking good is not always the same thing!

Q. My friend John wore a terrible shirt, it was checked and the colours did not match. His hair is like a cockatiel's. Is he a fashion disaster?

A. Depends on colours of checks & hair – C. Lacroix uses mismatched colours to great effect. If it didn't flatter John, however, then yes – fashion disaster!

Q. Is brown and black together wrong?

A. According to Askmen.com, black and brown are hard colours to combine. But acc to DKNY 2005 winter fashion: Black and Brown is a Striking Combination!

Q. The name DKNY, Donna Karan New York – is it 2 separate names or 1 name?

A. DKNY is the label of Donna Faske (born 2 October 1948 in Forest Hills, NY), better known as Donna Karan, a US fashion designer. Karan: her husband's surname.

Q. Was fashion icon Hugo Boss responsible for the design/styling of Nazi SS officers' uniforms?

A. During World War II, Mr Boss designed and manufactured uniforms and attire for troops, officers and other governmental Nazis including the SS.

Q. Which fashion designer was murdered on the order of his ex-wife?

A. Maurizio Gucci was shot down in front of his office in 1995. His ex-wife, Patrizia Reggiani, was arrested and charged with his murder in 1998.

Q. Which designer was murdered by Andrew in 1997?

A. On 15 July 1997, fashion designer Gianni Versace was shot dead in Miami by Andrew Phillip Cunanan. He committed suicide 8 days later.

Q. Who was the first fashion designer to release a fashion-related fragrance?

A. In 1911, Paul Poiret released the first designer perfume Martine, which was named after his second daughter.

Q. Is the designer Ralph Lauren a man or a woman?

A. Ralph Lauren is a male American fashion designer. Ralph Lauren was born Ralph Lipschitz on 13 October 1939.

Q. When was designer Paul Smith born exactly?

A. Sir Paul Smith: born 5 July 1946. Born in Nottingham, England. He only took up fashion design after having been injured in a cycling accident

———

Q. I'm a transvestite and I'm feeling a bit down today. I'm gonna get dressed up in a sexy outfit and spend the day shopping. Can you help me pick what to wear?

A. Something to make a girl feel good again. We suggest wearing shocking pink or red underwear, silk or satin are good as they feel nice next to skin. Make sure your shoes are comfortable!

Q. Were Mr T's gold chains on the 'A Team' real?

A. Apparently the jewellery worn on the 'A Team' was real. At one point, his gold chains, rings and bracelets were worth about USD 300,000. It took Mr T about an hour to put it on!

Q. What is known as a bum freezer?

A. A bum freezer is a jacket or jersey that's too short.

Q. What colour of pants am I wearing?

A. White has been the most popular colour for underwear ever since the 1950s. Therefore, your pants are statistically most likely to be white.

Q.   On average how many thongs does a
      woman own?

A.   Less than they used to! In recent years
      thong sales have declined to only 20 per
      cent of the market from a high of 31 per
      cent. Women own on average 22 pairs,
      suggesting 4–5 thongs.

———

Q.   My toenails have gone brown due to fake
      tan. How can I remove the stain?

A.   Try ¼ cup of lemon juice and ¼ cup of sugar.
      Mix them together and put them on the
      stained nails. Leave it on for about 5
      minutes as it needs to dry.

———

Q.   Why do women look sexy in just a football
      shirt?

A.   'Football? It's the beautiful game,' as
      Brazilian football legend Pele once said. So
      beautiful women & beautiful game = higher
      power beauty all round!

General Knowledge Questions 2

Q. Where in London can I get real bone from a hip and a jaw – animal or human?

A. Smithfield Market is your best place to pick up stray bones as it's home to many fine old-fashioned butchers.

Q. Is it possible 2 remove a human heart using only a spoon?

A. It would be possible provided the spoon was solid enough and the person cutting had enough strength and patience. Unless a coroner, it would be illegal.

Q. Is God ever angry?

A. In the Old Testament, God was angry when he destroyed the unbelievers in the flood. He seemed to mellow in the New Testament – perhaps it was fatherhood?

Q. **What percentage of the world's human population are f***wits (i.e. can't create truly original thoughts)?**

A. There are of course no stats on this, but as the old joke goes, 'They make themselves known by going to support Man Utd every week!' (Alter team to suit.)

Q. **What are the main differences between Marx and Weber's socialist theories?**

A. Marx argued that revolution of the proletariat was inevitable but Weber disagreed, asserting that ideology can act independently of economic conditions.

Q. What are the four amino acid motifs that form the replication associated protein needed for rolling circle replication and what are their functions?

A. E. coli Rep (replication associated protein) is a ssDNA helicase & has 4 domains: 1A, 1B & 2A (which bind ssDNA & ATP/ADP) & 2B (which may be regulatory).

Q. Is there a way to induce synaesthesia?

A. Yes, it is possible to induce synaesthesia. The CIA experimented with the use of LSD, which is known to induce synaesthesia.

Q. What exponent of Cartesian dualism proclaimed that there is no difference between the extended and the unextended?

A. The answer to this famous *Monty Python* quiz show sketch question (featuring Mrs Scum) is French philosopher Henri Bergson.

Q. Will monkeys ever be our masters?

A. The 1968 film (and 2001 remake) *Planet Of The Apes* predict a society ruled by monkeys. In reality it is accepted humans evolved from monkeys so is unlikely.

Q. What is the way to Amarillo from Westbury in Wiltshire avoiding motorways?

A. The way from Westbury, Wiltshire, to Amarillo, Texas, avoiding all motorways would be from your local airport, flying over the Atlantic for 4,720 miles.

Q. How much does it cost me on my electricity bill to boil my kettle?

A. A 3000 watt kettle typically boils in 6 minutes (0.1 hours). This is 0.3 kWh of electricity and currently costs about 1.7p in UK (at 5.5p per kWh).

Q.   If toast always lands butter-side down, what happens if I only use margarine?

A.   Bread lands butter-side down as size and shape of a piece of bread tends to make it rotate 180° as it falls off a table. The topping is inconsequential.

Q.   How many cows could be packed into the old and new Wembley Stadium?

A.   The new Wembley encloses 4 million cubic metres and a typical cow displaces 0.635 cubic metres. A good estimate would be a whopping 6.3 million cows!

Q.   Is 'What question is its own answer?' its own answer and, if not, why not?

A.   'Which question is its own answer?' is not its own answer as the question, whilst giving an answer, does not give the asked-for answer. Weird but true!

Q. **How many marbles would it take to stuff an adult elephant?**

A. A typical marble is 1cm³. If an African elephant's main body is 1.5m high, 1m wide and 3m long then it has a volume that holds 4.5 million marbles.

———

Q. **How many hoola hoops, standing on top of each other, would it take to reach the Moon?**

A. A hula hoop crisp is on average 1cm high, the Moon is 384,400km from earth. It would take 38,440,000,000 stacked to reach the Moon. Hope you're hungry!

———

Q. **What is the aristocrats joke?**

A. Comedian makes vile joke about family talent act audition. Many versions of joke, ends: Agent: 'Hell of an act. What do you call it?' Father: 'The Aristocrats!'

Q.   **Why is April the cruellest month?**

A.   T S Eliot: April breeds 'Lilacs out of the
      dead land, mixing/ Memory and desire'; he
      means spring is not yet here but signs make
      its absence more painful.

Q.   **Why don't good theories work?**

A.   Most theory evolves from hypotheses; many
      hypotheses turn out to be false. If a
      good/interesting theory is based on false
      hypotheses then it won't work.

Q.   **Who made God?**

A.   Both Scripture and logic testify to the fact
      that God is eternal. He had no origin. He is
      the everlasting I AM. No one 'made' him.
      He simply IS.

Q. We're ruminating over a good collective noun for nerds. What're your suggestions?

A. Suggestions for a collective noun for nerds: a trekkie of nerds, an academia of nerds, a calculation of nerds, a computation of nerds, a tedium of nerds.

———

Q. Can energy be destroyed?

A. Our fundamental laws of physics state that energy cannot be created or destroyed, only converted into/from matter. Energy/matter is a universal constant.

———

Q. How many licks does it take to get to the centre of a Tootsie Pop?

A. In separate scientific studies, two using robot tongues and two with humans, it has taken 364, 411, 252 or 144 licks to get to the centre of a Tootsie Roll.

Q. Tell me six interesting things.

A. Hummingbirds can't walk; Walt Disney, the creator of Mickey Mouse, was afraid of mice; the largest diamond ever found was an astounding 3,106 carats; the earth gets heavier each day by tons, as meteoric dust settles on it; koalas are excellent swimmers; a peanut is not a nut.

Q. When was the term zombie first used?

A. Zombie was first recorded in English as Zambi in an 1819 history of Brazil. It referred to an Angolan god spoken of by immigrant speakers of Kongo.

Q. How much does it cost to get a mail-order bride?

A. Agencies that can introduce you to foreign 'mail-order brides' have fees as little as £35 a month, and can have the whole process done for £2,500.

Q. **Know any good alcohol rehab centres near Glasgow that are cheap?**

A. Hillock's of Uplawmoor, G78 4AX, have varied fees depending on treatment, whereas Alcoholics Anonymous meet at the Baltic Chambers, and provide a free service.

———

Q. **Please enlighten me with some obscure names of beer.**

A. Strange beer names include Titanic Brewery's Lifeboat Ale, Marin Brewing's Bluebeery, Arrogant Bastard Ale, Old Leghumper, Skull Splitter, Erin Go Braless.

———

Q. **Why a Slippery Nipple is named as such?**

A. A correctly made Slippery Nipple looks like a nipple when viewed from above, hence the name. It's usually Bailey's with a drop of Sambuca (the nipple).

Q.   Yobs have thrown raw eggs on the front of my house. What's the best way to get rid of the mess?

A.   Hose off the area thoroughly as soon as you spot it. Remove excess egg and shells from the house using a towel and a cleaning solution made of one-half white vinegar and one-half warm water.

———

Q.   Where can I buy a fresh ostrich egg for cooking?

A.   An ostrich egg takes around one hour to boil and will happily feed 10! Call Ostrich Online on UK +44 1625 432462 for your nearest farm.

———

Q.   What is a great hangover cure?

A.   SoYouWanna.com Hangover Cure: 2 aspirins, 200mg cysteine, 600mg vitamin C, 1 vitamin B. Drink: banana, Red Bull, 6 strawberries, honey, orange juice, milk, salt, nutmeg.

Q. **Why are some crisps green, and should you eat them?**

A. Caused by light getting to potatoes after peeled but before cooked. Chlorophyll forms, giving the crisp a greenish hue. They taste bitter but aren't poisonous.

Q. **What is clinophobia?**

A. Clinophobia: abnormal & persistent fear of going to bed. The term is derived from the Greek '*klinein*' (to bend, slope or incline) and '*phobos*' (fear).

Q. **What is the fear blennophobia?**

A. Blennophobia is the morbid fear of slime. Myxophobia means the same thing. Not good phobias for Saturday-morning kids' TV hosts to have!

Q. **What is anti-climb paint?**

A. Anti-climb paint is a thick, non-drying coating for window sills, fencing and walls, etc. It is a deterrent to intruders as it is slippery and unclimbable.

Q. **What is the height of your average post box?**

A. The UK pillar box is usually around 5 feet 3 inches to 5 feet 4 inches. There are approximately 156 recognised designs and varieties of pillar boxes and wall boxes.

Q. **What is the distance around the Monopoly board in real life?**

A. To visit in order all of the London Monopoly properties (excluding stations and utilities) it is a distance of 12.83 miles between sites.

Q.   Is there a drink called the Sour Toe in the
     pub Downtown Motel in Dawson City,
     Canada and is it made with a real human
     toe?

A.   In Dawson, the Sour Toe of the North is a
     human toe. For 5 US dollars, you can put
     the toe in your cocktail, drink then swill
     down until the toe touches your lip.

_____

Q.   What is the name of the pub in 'Pop Goes
     the Weasel'?

A.   The pub in 'Pop Goes the Weasel' is the
     Eagle. The Eagle was a London pub, near
     the City Road, and a later Eagle pub still
     exists on the site.

_____

Q.   Given that I get through 7 tins of tuna a
     week, how many whole fish is this a year?

A.   Typical tuna size is about 500kg. Assuming
     typical tin of tuna 135g drained weight, you
     would consume 49.14kg of tuna a year,
     about one-tenth of a tuna.

Q. **Tell me some funny fake facts about David Hasselhoff?**

A. Funny fake facts about the Hoffmeister: he is a lesbian, he bathes iguanas in creosote for extra cash, he once dated a puma called Ethel, his mum is Lulu.

———

Q. **Who was the first person to eat broccoli?**

A. Broccoli is part of the cabbage family and is a hybrid developed in Taiwan. First person to eat it would have been a Taiwanese broccoli developer!

———

Q. **What happens to the extra soil once the coffin has gone into the soil? Obviously some of it fills the hole but there would be an excess so what happens to it?**

A. When a grave has been filled (after coffin placed in it), excess soil is distributed between existing graves and gardens within the cemetery.

Q. **Do you think we'll ever see a (real) Jurassic Park (à la the 1993 Speilberg movie) theme park? Could dinosaurs, t. rex, pterodactyls etc. be 'created' by fossilised DNA or DNA from existing reptilian life from 21st-century planet earth?**

A. After finding DNA of a zebra-like creature and attempting to clone it & bring it back from extinction, scientists believe progress can be made. Someday.

———

Q. **What's the best way to celebrate finishing exams?**

A. A skydive will probably be the best thing you do this summer, and is a hell of a way to celebrate your exams finishing!

Q.   **Who would win in a 200 metre sprint –
      Gordon Ramsay or David Hasselhoff?**

A.   Gordon Ramsey is the younger and fitter of
      the two, running annually in the London
      Marathon. He'd win, especially as The Hoff
      only ever runs in slow-mo!

———

Q.   **What do you do about liars in the office –
      what's the best put down?**

A.   The best way to put down a liar is to expose
      their lies. Make sure it is done in front of
      everyone for maximum effect.

———

Q.   **What's in a Pink Pussy?**

A.   A Pink Pussy is a cocktail containing 30ml
      white rum, 15ml strawberry schnapps, 15ml
      Malibu, 10ml grenadine and 80ml milk. It's
      also known as a Paxman!

Strange-but-true Facts

Q.   Which border are Border collies named after?

A.   The Border collie is descended from British droving breeds originating on the Scottish and English border, hence the name.

Q.   How much does a sheep cost to buy?

A.   A sheep costs approx £2.50 per lb. Average weight of a sheep is 150lbs. Average cost would therefore be £375. Best place to buy one is at a farmers' auction.

Q.   Where does the term hat-trick come from?

A.   Hat-trick comes from cricket; when a bowler took 3 wickets in a row he went around collecting money in a hat in recognition of good work.

Q. **Is it true that giraffes are incapable of making any vocal sounds?**

A. The belief that giraffes make no noise is a tall tale! They're quiet animals, and communicate with infrasonic sound, but they also make bleating sounds, similar to a young calf or sheep. They can make moaning, snoring, hissing, whistling, coughing, and flute-like sounds.

———

Q. **Why do people yawn?**

A. A yawn is an involuntary respiratory reflex, which regulates the carbon dioxide and oxygen levels in the blood.

———

Q. **Where does the saying 'frog in your throat' come from?**

A. Frog in the throat means suffering from temporary hoarseness – needing to clear the throat. It comes from the Old English '*frogga*' meaning hoarse.

Q.   How many people die from rabies annually?

A.   Rabies is responsible for between 50,000 and 70,000 deaths around the world each year, but the last UK death from the disease was in 1902.

Q.   How come superglue does not stick to the inside of the tube?

A.   Domestic glues work on the principle that they only become adhesive after prolonged contact with air. This is why glue around the top of bottles hardens.

Q.   Where did the term 'posh' originate from?

A.   Perhaps from the Romany word for 'dandy'; no evidence that it comes from 'port out starboard home' (the comfortable accommodation on ships between England and India).

Q. Who invented the drinks can?

A. In 1963, Ermal Fraze of Dayton, Ohio invented the integral rivet and ring-pull tab for opening a can and received US patent No. 3,349,949.

Q. Do puffins lose their beaks?

A. In winter, puffins shed the shell of their famous colourful beaks, to reveal a smaller, darker-coloured beak.

Q. Who is the oldest person alive?

A. Since August 27, 2006 the title-holder is Elizabeth Bolden of the USA. She was born on August 15, 1890 and is aged 116 as of August 2006.

Q. How do they get the bubbles in a bar of Aero?

A. The chocolate is cooked very quickly so bubbles remain resulting in 'igneous chocolate,' which is named after quickly-heated igneous rocks.

Q. Is the state where Jack Daniels is made a dry state?

A. Moore County, Tennessee, JDs' distillery, is one of the state's many dry counties. It is legal to distil the product within the county but illegal to buy it.

Q. What determines the queen bee to become queen?

A. When a queen dies or is lost, the worker bees pick out a few young worker larvae & feed them special royal jelly. These larvae then develop into queens.

Q. Has anyone ever been born with two willies?

A. Diphallia is a condition in which a male infant is born with two penises. It's estimated that 1 out of 5 million live births have this birth defect.

Q. When was the first leap year and who decided we needed it?

A. Gregorian calendar (current standard calendar) is a version of Roman Julian calendar, which had a leap year. It predates the 5th century BC.

Q. Do pineapples grow on trees?

A. It is a common misconception that pineapples grow on trees this is not true – pineapples are bromellicae and they grow on bush type plants.

Q. **Is it true that elephants die after their 6th set of teeth wear out?**

A. Elephants replace their back molars 6 times throughout life. When the last set of molars wears out, the elephant can no longer chew food and dies of starvation.

Q. **How many people can fit on the Isle of Wight?**

A. Isle of Wight is 380km in area. Approx 2.7636 thousand million people could stand in this area. This is just over a third of the world's population.

Q. **Where does the word 'quid' originate?**

A. The origins of the term for £1 are obscure – it possibly derives from the Latin 'Quid Pro Quo' meaning favour given in return for something, or simply quid 'that which is'.

Q. **How many bones are there in the body?**

A. At birth the body has about 350 bones, but by the time we reach adulthood, some bones have fused together to give us a total of 206 bones.

Q. **Where do swans sleep?**

A. Swans can sleep on land or water. They can sleep standing on one leg or whilst floating, usually with their heads tucked back under a wing.

Q. **Which animal has the longest pregnancy and how long is it?**

A. The longest gestation period for any animal is that of the spiny dogfish, *Squalus acanthias*, at 22–24 months.

Q. **What does 'sudoku' actually mean?**

A. Japanese company Nikoli introduced Sudoku to Japanese readers in 1984. The name 'sudoku' is the Japanese abbreviation of a longer phrase, '*Suuji wa dokushin ni kagiru*', meaning 'the digits must remain single'.

Q. **Where does the middle finger swear sign come from?**

A. Despite the belief that 'the finger' gesture originated in the battle of Agincourt, sexual gestures involving the middle finger are thousands of years old. They have been mentioned several times in the literature of ancient Rome.

Q. **Where do garden gnomes originate from and when did they first appear in the UK?**

A. The 1st garden gnomes were made in Germany in the mid-1800s. They 1st appeared here in 1847 when Sir Charles Isham brought 21 back from a trip to Germany.

———

Q. **When were contact lenses invented?**

A. German physiologist Adolf Eugen Fick constructed and fitted the first successful contact lens in 1887. They were made of heavy brown glass, and not comfy.

———

Q. **What is glass made from and how is it made?**

A. Natural glass has existed since the beginnings of time. It is made of silica (sand), soda & lime. The earliest man-made glass dates back to around 3500BC.

Q. **What was the original music chart based on?**

A. The singles chart was not born until November 1952 and it was based on sheet music sales. It was not until 1969 that a truly reliable chart emerged.

Q. **Where does the phrase 'Gordon Bennett' come from?**

A. Origin believed to come from James Gordon Bennett II (1841–1918) when he flew a plane through a barn. The name became synonymous with disbelief.

Q. Why do you never see baby pigeons?

A. Pigeons only lay 2 eggs at a time so the parents spoil the babies. The baby pigeons (squabs) do not leave the nest until they are almost fully grown.

Q. What is the rarest disease?

A. According to Guinness World Records, the world's rarest disease is smallpox which was eradicated in 1979, although cultures of the virus are held in the US and Russia.

Q. How big was Rasputin's penis?

A. In the UK, the average penis is 16cm (6.3 inches) long. The preserved penis of Rasputin is 30cm (11 inches). It's on display in St Petersburg, Russia.

Q. **What is the record of how many children a woman has given birth to?**

A. Mrs F Vassilyev (Russia, 1707–c.1782), gave birth to 69 children in 27 confinements (16 pairs of twins, 7 sets of triplets and 4 sets of quadruplets).

Q. **What does 'chav' mean?**

A. 'Chav' describes a young person, often without a high level of education, who follows a particular fashion.' It probably derives from the Romany word charvo for a child, and then used as a pejorative term for gypsy children. Some sources claim its origins are from 'Chatham girls'. Others say it's an acronym for council house and violent.

Q. **Where does the phrase 'the dogs bollocks' come from?**

A. The phrase 'The dogs' bollocks' was popularised by Viz magazine in 1989 and refers to a dogs' habit of licking the aforementioned organs in preference to almost any other activity.

Q. **If you tied buttered toast to the back of a cat and dropped it from a height, what would happen?**

A. The cat would land on its feet. Cats can twist in mid-air to ensure that they land feet down. Toast only has mythical power to land butter-side down.

Q. **What is the origin of the saying 'the bees knees'?**

A. A bee's corbiculae (pollen basket) is located on its tibiae & not actually knees! Phrase popularised in US in 1920s, possibly as a corruption of 'business'.

Q. **Why are cabs in America yellow?**

A. John Hertz decided that the secret to success in the cab biz was visibility. His research found yellow was the strongest colour to see at distance.

Q. **What is the speed of dark?**

A. The speed of dark: deduced speed is 98.9 ± 0.3 m/s. This is the time lag between turning off a laser and the arrival of dark.

Q. **What are the parent trees to the James Grieve apple?**

A. James Grieve is an old variety of apple, named after its breeder, James Grieve. It's a cross between a Pott's Seedling and a Cox's Orange Pippin. Sweet!

———

Q. **Wool shrinks in the wash – do sheep shrink in the rain?**

A. It requires both water AND heat to make wool shrink; that coupled with natural oils in the wool prevent sheep from shrinking in the rain.

———

Q. **How much does a Boeing 747 weigh?**

A. The Boeing 747 weighs 247,212kg (545,000lbs) empty, and has a maximum take-off weight of around 800,000lbs (Science Museum figures).

Q.   Where in the UK can I buy garlic ice cream (London if possible)?

A.   Garlic and Shots, 14 Frith Street, Soho, London gets great reviews. Their garlic ice cream costs £3.95 a bowl.

———

Q.   Which US astronaut has spent least time walking on the Moon?

A.   Only 12 of the 100s of US astronauts walked on the Moon. Buzz Aldrin and Neil Armstrong spent the least time on the surface – only 2 hours 31 minutes 40 seconds!

———

Q.   Are there really purple carrots?

A.   Yes there are. Carrots were purple or pale-coloured in ancient times. Patriotic Dutch breeders used a mutant seed in 16th century to create an orange variety.

Q. **Why was Dolly the sheep so called?**

A. Dolly was created by Scottish scientist Ian Wilmut; her donor cell came from the udder of a six-year-old sheep, which reminded him of Dolly Parton!

Q. **What English 10-letter word can you type using just the top row of a 'QWERTY' keyboard?**

A. Appropriately, it's 'TYPEWRITER'. 'REPERTOIRE' is a far less ironic & entertaining alternative, with the added debate: is it an 'English' word?

Q. **What monk created sparkling wine?**

A. Although Dom Pérignon, the 17th Century cellarmaster of Hautuillers Abbey, didn't invent sparkling wines, he is widely acknowledged for greatly improving the process. The first commercial sparkling wine was produced in the Limoux area of Languedec about 1535.

Q.   Who (and when) invented the traffic
     light?

A.   The world's first traffic lights invented by
     J P Knight & installed near London's House
     of Commons (intersection of George and
     Bridge Streets) in 1868.

———

Q.   Why is it colder at the top of a mountain
     when it is closer to the sun (i.e. why is it
     colder at higher altitudes)?

A.   Due to expansional cooling, gas gets colder
     as it expands. Heat in sea-level air has to
     occupy a larger volume at altitude, so colder
     as spread thinner.

———

Q.   What does the '20' in '20-20 vision' mean?

A.   It refers to what a 'normal' human being
     should be able to see clearly when standing
     20 feet away from an eye chart.

Q.   Was there truly one woman who survived
     the sinking of not only the *Titanic*, but
     also both her sister ships, and if so what
     was her name?

A.   Violet Jessop served on all 3 Olympic class
     'White Star Line' ships (*Titanic*, *Britannic* &
     Olympic) during their collisions and survived
     to tell the tale!

———

Q.   When was the phrase 'to coin a phrase'
     first coined (and why)?

A.   The verb 'to coin' originally meant to mint a
     coin, and dates to 14th century. In late-16th
     century the term generalised, 'to create'.
     1940 saw specific usage of to coin a phrase.

———

Q.   What temperature is it in space?

A.   Empty space itself cannot have a temp. as it
     is a vacuum. Object that absorbs & emits
     radiation perfectly at earth's distance from
     sun will reach 7°C.

Q. **Why is most tonic water commonly called Indian tonic water?**

A. Tonic water was originally intended for consumption in India & has quinine in it as a prophylactic against malaria, so commonly known as Indian tonic water.

Q. **What is the furthest man-made object from earth?**

A. Voyager 1, launched from Cape Canaveral on 5/9/1977, is now the furthest man-made object from the earth. On Feb. 2005, Voyager 1 was 10.4 billion km from sun.

Q. **Please tell me where the expression 'a gooseberry' comes from when referring to an odd one in a group.**

A. In the old days gooseberry was one of the many euphemisms for the Devil, who was naturally not welcome in most company. Now an unwelcome third party.

Q. What's the chances of your luggage getting put on the wrong plane or going astray in general?

A. Most airlines will not publish statistics for delayed luggage. SAS Scandinavian Airlines has the best record, just 10 bags per 1,000, or 1 per cent.

Q. Do you get wetter running in the rain than standing still in the rain for the same amount of time?

A. Tests suggest the same levels of wetness achieved. When standing more time to get wet, when running more drops hit. Also depends on wind speed & direction.

Q. **What are the 17 types of apple in Magners?**

A. Magners cider apples: Michelin, Dabinett, Yarlington Mill, Bulmer's Norman, Tremlett's Bitter, Breakwell Seedling, Taylor's, Harry Master's Jersey, Medaille d'Or, Reine des Pommes, Ashton Bitter, Bramley's, Grenadier, Brown Thorn, Brown Snout, Vilberies & Improved Dove.

––––––

Q. **Where does the phrase 'ripped off' come from?**

A. The phrase 'rip off': 'to steal or rob' was first recorded around 1967 in black slang, but rip was prison slang for 'to steal' since 1904.

––––––

Q. **What does pikestaff mean?**

A. Pikestaff: the shaft/staff of a pike (a pike is an old kind of spear) or a walking stick tipped with a metal spike. The phrase 'plain as a pikestaff' means 'very obvious'.

Q. **How big is a parsec?**

A. The parsec (symbol pc) is a unit of length used in astronomy. A parsec is a distance of about 3.25 light years.

Q. **Who's grave is most visited?**

A. One of the most visited graves on earth would be the grave of JFK with 4 million a year. Elvis's grave attracts 650,000 a year.

Q. **What is a sexton?**

A. Sexton: employee or officer of a church who is responsible for the care and upkeep of church property and sometimes for ringing bells and digging graves.

Q.   **What is the difference between a wizard and a warlock?**

A.   Warlocks are, among historic Christian traditions, said to be the male equivalent of witches. So they may be wizards, but always evil ones.

———

Q.   **Why is Alcatraz no longer a running prison?**

A.   Alcatraz is no longer used due to the cost of running the prison, dilapidated conditions and pollution to the area caused by the prison.

———

Q.   **What is dark matter, and how is it created?**

A.   Dark Matter: hypothetical particles (unknown composition) do not reflect enough radiation to be detected but presence inferred from gravitational effects.

Q. **Does the US dollar bill contain any freemason symbols?**

A. Many symbols used on the US 1 dollar bill can be interpreted towards freemasonry, including the pyramid emblem with all-seeing eye, and the 32 feathers on the eagle.

———

Q. **What is the opposite of misogynist (i.e. woman who hates men)?**

A. Equivalent is misandrist (person who hates persons of male sex), rare word but seemingly much sought-after.

———

Q. **Was Ghandi ever thrown from a train and if so, by whom?**

A. Ghandi was thrown off train at Pietermaritzburg station, South Africa after he refused to move to a third-class carriage because of racial discrimination.

Q.   How does the Aquafresh toothpaste
     always come out in three colours and not
     mixed together?

A.   The different coloured toothpastes are
     arranged separately within the Aquafresh
     tube and patented nozzle system ensures all
     3 come out together.

Q.   Is it true you can't flush your toilet after
     10 p.m. on a Sunday night in Switzerland?

A.   In Switzerland, it is illegal to flush toilet after
     10 p.m. if you live in an apartment. Also,
     men may not relieve themselves while
     standing up, after 10 p.m.

Q.   Why are there extra pillars across the
     River Thames between Blackfriars Road
     & Rail Bridge?

A.   The pillars, which stand between the 2
     bridges, are what remains of another rail
     bridge opened in 1864 that carried the
     London Chatham & Dover Railway.

Q. **What does Mercedes AMG mean?**

A. AMG is from the original founders' initials: Hans-Werner Aufrecht & Erhard Melcher, as well as the town where Aufrecht was born, Grossaspach.

Q. **Who invented the pie chart?**

A. Pie charts can be traced back to 1801 but were made popular when, in 1858, Florence Nightingale used them during the Crimean War, to support her argument that more soldiers died from disease than in battle.

Q. **What does IC mean in police terms?**

A. In police terms, IC Codes are used to describe ethnic origin. 1 – White European, 2 – Dark European, 3 – Afro Caribbean, 4 – Asian (Indian), 5 – Asian (Oriental), 6 – Arab.

Q. What does 'white trash' mean?

A. 'White trash' is an American ethnic slur or racial epithet usually used to describe certain low-income persons of European descent.

———

Q. What is mechanically recovered chicken?

A. Mechanically recovered meat (MRM) is a purée of residual meat left on bones formed by forcing the meat/bone through a sieve at high pressure to separate.

———

Q. Did the Dalai Lama go to English public school?

A. Tenzin Gyatso (b. 6 July 1935) 14th and current Dalai Lama, grew up in a small and poor Tibetan settlement. He did not attend British public school.

Q. **Where does idea that counting sheep helps you get to sleep come from?**

A. To count sheep in a bid to induce sleep is recorded from 1854. Sheep-counting systems ultimately derive from the Cumbric language.

___

Q. **On average how many pints of beer are drunk in England in a weekend?**

A. The entire UK drinks approximately 1.3 pints per day per person, so over a 2-day weekend all of England would drink at least 157.15 million pints of beer.

___

Q. **In numerical format if you took a chess board and placed 1 grain of rice on the first square and kept doubling up how many would be on the 64th square?**

A. There would be approx 18,446,744,070,000,000,000 grains of rice on the last square of the chess board.

Q. If everybody in the world jumped at the same time would there be an earthquake?

A. In 2001, over a million people in the UK registered a 3 magnitude quake in the 'Giant Jump'. The entire world would thus give a small 5.5 magnitude quake.

Sports
Questions

Q.   How many decibels are recorded at the
     start of an F1 race?

A.   F1 can exceed 130db. This level of noise is
     above the average human pain threshold of
     120db.

———

Q.   Which four English players have cost
     7 million GBP or more, but never played
     for England?

A.   Four Premiership players have cost over
     7 million GBP or more and have never
     played for England: Dean Richards, Kevin
     Davies, Carl Cort, Dean Ashton.

———

Q.   Which game starts with a squidge off?

A.   Tiddlywinks starts with a squidge off. All
     players shoot one wink from their baseline
     towards the pot. The player landing closest
     to the pot wins.

Q. **Who was the first player to score a 5-point try in rugby union, against whom and when?**

A. The first player to score a 5-point try in rugby was Inga Tuigamala for New Zealand against Australia in Sydney in July 1992.

Q. **How many golf balls are on the moon?**

A. Apollo 14 (1971): Shepard, the first golfer on the moon, took 3 balls. He left a ball behind for future golfers.

Q. **Who has hit the fastest one-day hundred in cricket and how many balls did it take?**

A. Shahid Afridi holds the world record for fastest 1-day hundred of 37 balls v Sri Lanka in 1996.

Q. **Which player has played in London, Manchester and Merseyside derbies, won the FA cup, the Premiership, the Champions League and the European Championship?**

A. Nicolas Anelka has scored in all three derbies (Arsenal, Liverpool and Man City) and has won the FA Cup, Premiership and Champions League and the European Championships.

Q. **Is professional darts a sport or a game?**

A. Darts was officially listed in England as a pastime. As of June 2005 Sport England officially recognised darts as a sport as it involves skill over chance.

Q. How many different weight classes are there in boxing?

A. There are 17 weight classes in boxing – straw, junior fly, fly, junior bantam, bantam, junior feather, feather, junior light, light, junior welter, welter, junior middle, middle, super middle, light-heavy, cruiser and heavyweight.

———

Q. Name the Aussie wicketkeeper who took 366 catches before moving into commentary?

A. Ian Healy of Australia is the leading Test Match wicketkeeper. He dismissed 395 batsmen in 119 matches, 366 catches. Is currently a commentator.

Q.   **Which club provided the entire Scottish team v England in 1872?**

A.   Saturday, 30 November 1872: Scotland 0 England 0. First true international between Scotland and England, with Queens Park representing the Scots.

———

Q.   **When is a tennis ball at its fastest ... on racquet impact or when?**

A.   The tennis ball is at its fastest when it leaves contact with the racquet. It may slow by 50 per cent when it reaches the baseline at the other end of the court.

———

Q.   **Which two Premiership players' names are anagrams of each other?**

A.   Nolberto SOLANO of Newcastle United and Xavi ALONSO of Liverpool are anagrams of each other.

Q. **How many strawberries are consumed at Wimbledon during the tournament?**

A. Every day more than two tonnes of strawberries are eaten. Each year between 27 and 34 tonnes of strawberries are eaten during the entire tournament.

———

Q. **Which football manager failed an attempt to trademark his name?**

A. Oct. 2005: Man Utd boss Sir Alex Ferguson failed to ban posters bearing his name because he's 'too famous'. His lawyer is appealing under Human Rights Act.

———

Q. **Has there ever been a ref. sent off during the history of the World Cup games?**

A. No evidence of referee being sent off in World Cup, though Graham Poll played no further part in matches in 2006 World Cup after giving Šimunić three yellow cards! In a charity match, a ref. shot a player in the head for refusing to leave.

Q. Name four English league teams that have all five vowels in their name?

A. Only 3 current league teams have 5 vowels Hartlepool United, Torquay United and Rotherham United. Rushden & Diamonds were relegated in 2005/2006 and would have been the 4th team!

———

Q. Could ex *Neighbours* hard-case Joe Scully take Mike Tyson in a bare-knuckle fist fight?

A. Most likely Mike Tyson would win in a fight due to his previous background. Joe Scully recently featured in Sheila's Car Insurance ad.

———

Q. Why is Andrew Flintoff nicknamed Freddie?

A. Andrew 'Freddie' Flintoff MBE, picked up the nickname 'Freddie' or 'Fred' due to perceived similarities with Fred Flintstone.

Q. How many times does a footballer kick a football in his career?

A. Premiership player, no injuries. Start at age of 18, end at 34. League average 608 games, Cups average 100 games, non-competition average 100 = 808 total. 40 touches per match. 32,320 in career.

Q. Which footballer has played in the most World Cups?

A. There are two. Germany's Lothar Matthaus (1982, 1986, 1990, 1994 and 1998) and Antonio Carbajal of Mexico (1950, 1954, 1958, 1962, 1966) have played in 5 World Cups.

Q. Who was the fastest bowler to break 100mph? And what was Jeff Thomson's fastest ball?

A. Fast bowler Shoaib Akhtar became the 1st bowler to officially clock 100mph (160km/h) in international cricket in 2003. Jeff's fastest clocked at 99.7mph!

———

Q. What is the name of the cricket ground that has the tree on the pitch, which if you hit you get 4 runs.

A. The St Lawrence ground, Canterbury is home to Kent CCC. The lime tree that was on the pitch blew down in strong winds in 2005, but has been replanted since.

———

Q. How many ways are there to be out in cricket?

A. The 10 ways of getting out in cricket: caught, bowled, LBW, run out, stumped, hit wicket, handling the ball, double strike, obstruction and timed out.

Q. **What sport has the fastest travelling ball or puck, e.g. tennis, cricket?**

A. The fastest projectile speed in any moving ball game is approximately 302km/h (188mph) in jai-alai (Spanish sport like pelota).

Q. **Can an individual person represent a country at one sport then represent another country at another sport?**

A. Yes. For example, Henry Paul had played rugby league for New Zealand but was allowed to play rugby union for England as he had not played the sport in New Zealand.

Q. **What sport do you play backwards?**

A. Sports that you start and finish backwards: back-stroke swimming, rowing, diving and Tug of War, also some special running and skiing events.

Q.   Which sports use a net but no ball?

A.   Sports with a net but no ball: fishing,
     trampolining, ice hockey, badminton, discus
     and hammer throwing.

———

Q.   What is the longest foot race in the world?

A.   The Self-Transcendence 3,100-mile race is
     the world's longest foot race. It is hosted by
     the Sri Chinmoy Marathon Team and takes
     place in Queens, New York.

———

Q.   What's the world record for the longest
     tug of war?

A.   Slaughter Across the Water, Eastport USA is
     the longest tug of war over a body of water
     in the world. Features a 1,700ft rope and
     over 450 tuggers.

Q. **Which sport has produced the most winners of BBC1's Sports Personality of the Year?**

A. With 16 winners of the BBC Sports Personality Award, athletics is the most represented sport. Between 1980–87 there was always an athlete in the top 3!

———

Q. **How much does the fattest sumo wrestler in the world weigh?**

A. The world's heaviest athlete is sumo wrestler, Manny Yarborough (USA) – 6 ft 8 inches tall & 50 stone 4 lbs.

———

Q. **Who are the world Elephant Polo champions?**

A. The Chivas Regal Elephant Polo team of Scotland were 2005 World Elephant Polo champions beating the National Parks team from Nepal, 7–6, 27 Nov. 2005.

Q.   **What football team did Wet Wet Wet sponsor?**

A.   In the early 90s, Wet Wet Wet were the shirt sponsors of Clydebank FC. The band Mansum also gave money to Chester City FC a few years ago.

———

Q.   **Why don't Barcelona have a shirt sponsor?**

A.   In Catalonia, Barça are regarded by many as true 'national' team, and national teams have no shirt sponsor. Recent deal with Unicef because FC Barcelona is 'not only a football club, but a club with a soul.'

———

Q.   **Who is the most capped player in international football?**

A.   Saudi Arabian goalkeeper Mohammad Al-Deayea is the most capped player of all time. He has an amazing 183 caps for his country.

Q. **What was the highest scoring penalty shoot-out score?**

A. In the Jeux de la Francophonie, 2005, a match between Burkina Faso and Cameroon took at least 49 penalty kicks, with Burkina Faso emerging 25–24 winners.

––––––

Q. **Out of all the premiership managers, who would win in a fight?**

A. Allardyce (size/weight), & Redknapp (East End connections) are all contenders but wouldn't mix it with original 'psycho' Stuart Pearce.

––––––

Q. **Who would win in a fight between Zinedine Zidane and Roy Keane?**

A. Roy Keane & Zinedine Zidane both have bad disciplinary records. Keane is probably 'harder' as he allegedly deliberately ended A. I. Haaland's career.

Q. Why in tennis is a zero score called 'love'?
Why in tennis is the score 40–40 called
'deuce'?

A. Tennis scoring: 'deuce' is a corruption of
deux (two – 2 consecutive exchanges
needed to win); 'love' is from French word
l'oeuf (egg – 0).

———

Q. **How many balls are used during the
Wimbledon fortnight?**

A. In 2006, Slazenger supplied 52,200 tennis
balls to Wimbledon. About 20,000 of these
are used for qualifying and practice, so
32,200 for matches.

———

Q. **How many Grand Slam events has Tim
Henman won?**

A. Tim Henman has never won a Grand Slam
in tennis. His record: Australian 4R (2000,
2001, 2002), French SF (2004), Wimbledon
SF (1998, 1999, 2001, 2002), US SF (2004).

Q. **How many pro boxers have died in the boxing ring?**

A. According to an article from the journal of combative sport, 1,326 fatalities have occured in boxing history in the ring, as of April 2006.

———

Q. **Which sport is the more dangerous in terms of fatalities per year – cycling or horseracing?**

A. Several sources claim that horse racing is one of the most dangerous sports in the world, with around 5 deaths per year in the UK – so more dangerous than cycling.

———

Q. **Which animal out of a horse and a greyhound has gained the top speed?**

A. Horse is faster. American quarter horse can attain speeds of up to 55 miles per hour. Fastest greyhound time recorded is 39.87 miles per hour!

Q.   How many times taller are the UK's tallest rugby posts than those at Twickenham?

A.   Twickenham posts are 54 feet 2 inches high. Wednesbury RFC's posts are 126 feet high, around 2.3 times higher than Twickenham's.

Q.   How far could Tiger Woods hit a golf ball on the moon?

A.   US astronaut Shepard was first golfer on the moon in 1971. According to NASA, the balls went 2km. Woods would not drive much further – space suit is restrictive!

Q.   Who is the highest paid sports person in the world?

A.   Golf currently has the highest earning potential of all sports. Tiger Woods earns 45 million GBP a year and is the highest paid sportsman in the world.

Q.   **What is the most watched sport in the world?**

A.   Formula One racing is the most watched sport in the world. The estimated annual viewers (international television & at the race tracks) is 57 billion.

Q.   **How big would a snooker cue have to be in order to use it to 'pot the earth' into the nearest black hole? And how hard would you have to hit it?**

A.   A snooker ball is 52.5mm, a snooker cue is 1470mm. Earth's diameter is 12,756.3km, so cue would have to be 357,716.4km long. Nearest black hole 1600 light years away.

Q. **What is the purpose of the flat part on the side of a snooker cue near 2 the base of the cue?**

A. This is a classic tradition prior to the advent of rest handles, where the cue was used instead of a rest handle. The flat part of the cue allowed a player to lay the whole cue on the table and slide the cue to hit a ball that could not be reached.

Q. **Everton jokes?**

A. Joke about Everton fans: What is the difference between Everton FC and foot and mouth? Foot and mouth made it to Europe!

Q. **Another Everton joke – a really good one.**

A. Rumour has it that Everton have got a new sponsor: Tampax. The board thought it was an appropriate change as the club is going thru a very bad period.

Film and
Television
Questions

Q. What was the name of the poo used to move the Statue of Liberty in *Ghostbusters 2*?

A. In *Ghostbusters II*, 'mood slime' was used to animate the Statue of Liberty, as it could cause solid substances to animate.

Q. Who were He-Man's enemies apart from Skeletor?

A. He-Man battled Beast-Man, Mer-Man, Evil-Lyn, Tri-Klops, Trap Jaw, Faker (clone of He-Man), Panthor, Jitsu, Whiplash, Clawful, Kobra Klan and many more!

Q. What is the full sequence in *Trainspotting* when they say it's shite being Scottish you're the lowest of the low?

A. 'We're the lowest of the fucking low, the scum of the earth, the most wretched, servile, miserable, pathetic trash that was ever shat into civilisation.'

Q. Who is the 'mild-mannered Janitor' in
    Hong Kong Phooey?

A. Penrod Pooch (Penry for short) is a mild-
    mannered janitor at the police department.
    Unbeknownst to all but his cat, Spot, he's
    really Hong Kong Phooey!

————

Q. Who is the strongest James Bond of all
    time and in which film?

A. In *The World Is Not Enough*, Bond (played by
    Brosnan) opens an airlock underwater,
    fighting huge pressure. It's Bond's most
    impressive feat of strength.

————

Q. Can you tell me how to get how to get to
    Sesame Street, how to get to Sesame
    Street, how to get to Sesame Street?

A. *Sesame Street*, a kids' TV show, was first aired on
    10 Nov. 1969. It's a fictional place in NY City.
    Therefore we are unable to provide directions
    to it. It's got a subway station, though.

Q. Who is the Stig in *Top Gear*?

A. The Stig on *Top Gear* is usually ex-ASCAR driver Ben Collins although sometimes private owners are the Stig. The old Stig was ex-F1 driver Perry McCarthy.

———

Q. In the movie *Stand By Me,* what flavour pie in the pie-eating competition?

A. In the film *Stand By Me* the pie-eating contest is with blueberry pies. Strangely, all the spectators also vomit blueberries in this scene.

———

Q. What is the chocolate given to Sloth in the movie *The Goonies*?

A. In *The Goonies*, Chunk begins his friendship with Sloth by giving him a Baby Ruth chocolate bar. Chunk: 'You want a candy bar? I got a Baby Ruth, sir.'

Q. Who smashed up the *Blue Peter* garden?

A. The culprits were never identified. However, in 2000, footballer Les Ferdinand boasted that he was a member of the gang who trashed the *Blue Peter* garden.

Q. What's Bananaman's real human name?

A. In the comic, Bananaman had red gloves and was called Eric Wimp. On TV, his name was Eric Twinge and he had yellow gloves.

Q. Why is a Green Room (for theatre, TV etc.) so called?

A. A minor mystery! 1st recorded use in Thomas Shadwell's play *The True Widow*, debuted London 1678. May refer to actors' livery or baize that protected costumes.

Q.   In *The Simpsons,* how much younger is Milhouse than Bart Simpson?

A.   Milhouse Mussolini Van Houten is Bart Simpson's best friend, the son of Kirk and Luann Van Houten. He once stated he was 3 months younger than Bart.

───

Q.   How many DVDs have been released in England so far since their launch?

A.   There are over 100,000 DVD titles released since launch of the format due to foreign films and back catalogues being released as well.

───

Q.   Who won *Big Brother 2?*

A.   Brian Dowling (born 13 June 1978) was the winner of the second series of the British reality TV show *Big Brother* in 2001.

Q. Who sang the song in the *Only Fools and Horses* episode – the jolly boys outing?

A. In the jolly boys outing on *Only Fools and Horses*, songs played include 'Down Down' (Status Quo), '2-4-6-8 Motorway' (Tom Robinson Band) & 'Everybody's Talkin''.

———

Q. When Marge Simpson puts her daughter Maggie through the supermarket checkout in the opening credits, what flashes up on the till screen?

A. Maggie's scan has frequently been changed to 'No sale', but usually says $847.63 USD – once determined to be the monthly cost of raising a child in the US.

Q.   Why does Noel Edmonds have a different symbol on his hand every show on *Deal or No Deal*?

A.   According to the *Sun*, symbols on Noel Edmond's hands are for good luck (cosmic ordering). Last year, he wished for a hit show and a house abroad. He got both.

———

Q.   When will *Rocky 6* be released and what is the premise?

A.   *Rocky Balboa* (6th film) is scheduled for UK release on 9 Feb. 2007. Plot: hard up for money, retired Rocky comes back in the ring to fight champion.

———

Q.   Will George A. Romero be making any more zombie movies?

A.   George A. Romero has written *Diamond Dead* (unconfirmed as director) to be released in 2007. A woman resurrects a zombie rock band to kill 365 people.

Q. Is there going to be a second series of
    Supernatural – when will it be on British
    television?

A. On 18 May 2006, it was confirmed that
    Supernatural will be getting renewed for
    another series. No word yet on when it will
    air in Britain though.

———

Q. How many episodes of *Only Fools and
    Horses* have there been in total?

A. There were 79 episodes of *Only Fools and
    Horses* in all, 13 episodes being Christmas
    specials with 66 normal episodes in 9
    seasons.

———

Q. When did the *Spiderman* TV show
    cartoon start first in the 60s?

A. Spiderman first appeared in *Amazing Fantasy*
    #15 (Aug. 1962; comic book). The cartoon
    TV-series appeared between 1967–1970.
    22 min. (52 episodes, 52 min.)

Q.   What nude scenes has Jennifer Connelly done?

A.   Jennifer Connelly has done several nude scenes, including: *Requiem for a Dream*, *Waking the Dead*, *The Hot Spot*, *Inventing the Abbotts*, *House of Sand and Fog*.

Q.   How much of Jennifer Aniston do you see in film *The Break-up* and for how long?

A.   All reports only say that you see her naked from behind, for less than 1 scene.

Q.   When was first show of *Hong Kong Phooey* on TV?

A.   *Hong Kong Phooey* is a 16-episode (31 shorts) Hanna-Barbera animated series that first aired in 1974.

Q. **What per cent of the vote did Grace get in *Big Brother* for eviction?**

A. *Big Brother* Day 30: Grace was the 4th person to be evicted from the *Big Brother* house with 87.9 per cent of the vote.

Q. **When did *Batfink* first appear?**

A. *Batfink* 5-minute shorts were first aired in Sept. 1967; then aired throughout 80s; and revived between 1995–1997. In April 2006 they enjoyed another repeat run on BBC 2.

Q. **Has anyone won *Deal or No Deal?***

A. The most ever won on *Deal or No Deal* is 2 million Australian dollars on their version. As of 21.4.06, the most ever won in the UK version is £120,000.

Q. **When did Mighty Mouse first appear?**

A. Mighty Mouse was created as a parody of Superman, and he first appeared in 1942 in a theatrical animated short entitled *The Mouse of Tomorrow*.

Q. **What species is Yoda from *Star Wars*?**

A. George Lucas has never given a species name for Yoda. So, at present, the answer is 'species unknown.'

Q. **What species was Darth Maul from *Star Wars*?**

A. Darth Maul, a fictional character from *Star Wars Episode 1*, is of the Zabrak race, humanoids whose most distinctive feature are their small horns.

Q. **How many actors have played Doctor Who?**

A. 10 actors have played Dr Who on television: William Hartnell, Patrick Troughton, Jon Pertwee, Tom Baker, Peter Davison, Colin Baker, Slyvester McCoy, Paul McGann, Christopher Eccleston & David Tennant. He was played by Peter Cushing in the 1960s movies, by Richard E. Grant in online eposides and Richard Hurndall portrayed the first Doctor in The Five Doctors after Hartnell's death.

———

Q. **In the TV programme *Kung Fu* are the actor David Carradine's dragon and tiger tattoos real?**

A. Although we can't find conclusive proof, the tattoos Kwai Chang Caine (David Carradine) sports in *Kung Fu: The Legend Continues* appear to be fake.

Q.   Do you whistle while you work?

A.   'Whistle While you Work' is the famous
     song that was sung by the seven dwarfs in
     the famous 1937 Disney animated feature,
     Snow White and the Seven Dwarfs.

———

Q.   Who shot JR?

A.   80 per cent of American viewers saw the
     Dallas episode that solved the 'Who Shot
     JR?' mystery on 21 Nov. 1980 (it was his
     pregnant lover, Kristin Shepherd).

———

Q.   How many more series of *24* are they
     going to make?

A.   Season 6 of the Fox TV series *24* returns to
     Monday nights in January 2007 in the USA.
     A feature film will follow, which will
     hopefully be followed by a seventh season.

Q. From the TV show *The Simpsons,* there is a character named Cletus (the hillbilly character). Can you name his children?

A. Tiffany, Heather, Cody, Dylan, Dermot, Jordan, Taylor, Brittany, Wesley, Rumor, Scout, Cassidy, Zoe, Clo, Max, Hunter, Kendall, Caitlin, Noah, Sasha, Morgan, Kyra, Ian, Lauren, Q-bert, Phil, Rubella and Candaleeza Marie.

Q. Which films does Tara Reid get naked in?

A. No naked shots in movies but Tara Reid exposed her left breast when her dress fell at P. Diddy's 35th birthday party at Cipriani's restaurant in New York.

Q. **What is the song on the Sony advert with all the bouncy calls?**

A. Sony Bravia liquid crystal TV advert – used 250,000 bouncy rubber balls fired out of cannons. The song is Jose Gonzalez's acoustic cover of 'Heartbeats' originally by The Knife.

———

Q. **Which film used the catchphrase 'Don't get mad, get even'?**

A. *Animal House* is the film that has that famous quote. It was made in 1978 starring John Belushi and Tim Matheson.

———

Q. **What is the connection between *Postman Pat* and *Lord of the Rings*?**

A. Both *Postman Pat* and *Lord of the Rings* were inspired by British beauty spots – Longsleddale and the Ribble Valley respectively.

Q. **What's that invention called that aids you to run on the advert for Zurich Insurance?**

A. Those springy stilt-things are called Powerisers. They are available from www.streetgadgets.com for around £200. Comprehensive health insurance recommended!

———

Q. **Who won *Celebrity Big Brother* 2005?**

A. Bez won the 2005 *Celebrity Big Brother*. He is famous for being the Happy Mondays' dancer/maraca player.

———

Q. **What happened to the A Team van?**

A. One of the original six vans used for the show is displayed in the Cars of the Stars Motor Museum in Keswick.

Q. **Did Wile E. Coyote ever catch the Roadrunner?**

A. Roadrunner never gets caught by Wile E. Coyote. In episode 'Soup Or Sonic' Wile appears to make the catch, but Roadrunner is at the time gigantic & escapes.

Record
Questions

Q. How many women has 007 slept with, in total, in all the Bond films?

A. Between *Dr No* and *Die Another Day*, Bond has slept with 44 women in the official films. Three-quarters of these women have also attempted to kill Bond!

Q. What is the most amount of men a woman has slept with in one go in the Guinness World Records?

A. According to Guinness World Records, Annabel Chong (at age 22) had sex 251 times with 80 guys in a 1995 stunt filmed for *Sex: The Annabel Chong Story*.

Q. Who is the loveliest of them all?

A. According to askmen.com, Adriana Lima (Brazilian supermodel) is the most desirable woman in the world for British men.

Q. **Who is the most beautiful girl in London?**

A. Beauty is in the eye of the beholder, but in 2005 *FHM* readers voted *EastEnders'* Michelle Ryan the 4th sexiest woman in the world – top scoring Londoner.

Q. **How long is the longest pubic hair ever?**

A. The longest pubic hair in history was recorded by midwife (no name) in the 19th century. The woman's hair grew beyond her knees and was 'plaited behind her back'.

Q. **How tall is the smallest ever adult human male?**

A. The shortest ever adult male (and shortest human) was Gul Mohammed of India. On 19 July 1990 he was measured at 57cm.

Q.   Who earns the most money in the world?

A.   Bill Gates' net worth is around $46.6 billion, which makes him the world's richest person – he approximately earns 300 dollars per second!

———

Q.   How young was the youngest person ever to have a baby?

A.   Youngest mother whose history is authenticated is Lina Medina, delivered 6-pound boy by caesarean section in Lima, Peru in 1939, age 5 years, 7 months.

———

Q.   What is the fastest recorded time for a pantomime horse to finish the London Marathon?

A.   Fastest time for a pantomime horse in marathon is 4 hours 37 minutes. Fastest 100m is 13.51 seconds by Charles Astor and Tristan Williams in 2005.

Q. **Who is the biggest female porn star?**

A. In 2005 Adult Film Fan Porn Star Awards, Ariana Jollee won the award for Top Porn Star. Other suggestions – Jenna Jameson and Tera Patrick.

———

Q. **Which family has won the most Oscars for acting? And overall (director, writing, music score etc.)?**

A. The Coppolas: Carmine, Best Music (1974); Francis Ford, Best Writing (1970, 1972, 1974); Best Director (1974) & Best Picture (1974); Sofia, Best Writing (2003).

———

Q. **What film has lost the most money ever?**

A. According to the Razzie's *Swept Away* is the lowest grossing movie of recent years. Starring Madonna, it grossed $598,645 of $10 million it took to make.

Q. **What was the longest sex session?**

A. Longest lovemaking session, Mae West (1892–1980). In her autobiography, she writes of how she & a sexual prodigy named Ted made love for 15 consecutive hours.

Q. **What is the name of the biggest organism on the planet?**

A. In 2000, a fungus growing through the earth in the Malheur National Forest E. Oregon, covering 890 hectares of land was found – this is largest organism found.

Q. **How big is the biggest human penis in the world?**

A. Largest penis found in Kinsey Report was 9.5 inches. Dr David Ruben reported 14-inch penis, but not verifiable. Porn star John Holmes's penis allegedly 12 inches.

Q. Who has the biggest natural boobs in the world?

A. According to Guinness World Records, Norma Stitz currently holds the record for the largest natural breasts. They weighed approximately 28lbs each & she was a size 48V at the time.

Q. What is most expensive vibrator in the world?

A. World's most expensive vibrator cost $1500.00 US. Developed by Lelo Company of Sweden it includes a wooden box and satin carry pouch and is made of golden metal.

Q. How many doors are there in the White House?

A. The White House has 412 doors. It is 6 storeys and 5100m^2 of floor space, with 132 rooms and 35 bathrooms, 147 windows and 28 fireplaces.

Q.   **What is the hardest question to answer ever, and what is the answer?**

A.   The world's hardest question to answer has previously been claimed to be 'Does my bum look big in this?' Any response is bound to get you in trouble!

Q.   **What is the most amount of toes a person ever had?**

A.   The person with the most fingers and toes is Devendra Harne (India born, 9.1.95) who has 12 fingers & 13 toes as a result of the condition polydactylism.

Q.   **What is the world record for the largest gingerbread man ever baked?**

A.   According to the Guinness World Records, the world's largest gingerbread man weighed a whopping 168.8kg & was made by chefs at the Hyatt Regency Hotel, Vancouver, Canada, on 19 November 2003.

Q. **Where is the sunniest place on Earth?**

A. According to Guinness World Records, the annual average in Yuma, Arizona, USA is 91 per cent of the possible hours of sunshine (4,055 hours of 4,456 hours in a year).

Historical
& Political
Questions

Q.   **What playing card is the 'Curse of Scotland'?**

A.   The 'Curse of Scotland' is a term applied to the nine of diamonds. The phrase, first recorded in the early 18th century, has many colourful explanations. Many bridge and poker players swear it relates to a game called Pope Joan, in which the nine of diamonds is the Pope – the anti-Christ to Scottish Presbyterians and Reformers.

Q.   **Who shot JFK?**

A.   The official response is that Lee Harvey Oswald shot JFK on November 22nd 1963 but an ABC News poll found that 68 per cent of the US believes there was a cover-up.

Q.   **Why does a kamikaze pilot wear a helmet?**

A.   Simply put, the helmet was necessary to pilot the aircraft. Inside the helmet was the communication gear, and the goggles were attached to helmet as well.

Q. Who is the worst person who has ever lived?

A. This is a completely subjective answer but Chairman Mao, Hitler, Stalin and Pol Pot are directly and indirectly responsible for the deaths of over 75 million people.

Q. What are the Four Horsemen of the Apocalypse?

A. The Four Horsemen of the Apocalypse (from the Book of Revelation, the last book in the Bible) are widely believed to be War, Famine, Pestilence and Death. Death is the only 'horseman' specifically stated and some believe that the four horsemen are actually conquest, war, famine and death.

Q. **What was the name of the first dog launched into space?**

A. On November 3rd 1957, Sputnik 2 was launched carrying a dog named Laika. Laika was the first animal to orbit the earth and died just hours after launch.

———

Q. **What is the Domesday Book?**

A. The Domesday Book, also known as the Book of Winchester, was a census of England taken in the 11th century.

———

Q. **Why are American Indians called Indians?**

A. When Columbus landed in the New World (South America), he called the people Indians because he wrongly believed he had reached the Indies (medieval Asia). Even so, the name stuck.

Q.   What is America named after?

A.   America derives its name from the Italian
     explorer Amerigo Vespucci; in 1507, Martin
     Waldseemaller published a world map calling
     the New World (both continents) America.

———

Q.   How many landings have there been on
     the moon?

A.   There were 6 successful moon landings
     between 1969–1972. There have been 12
     different people on moon.

———

Q.   Who was involved in the shortest war in
     history and how long did it last?

A.   The shortest war is history is the British
     invasion of Zanzibar at 9:00 am on August
     27th 1896. At 9:45 am Zanzibar
     surrendered!

Q. **Which pin-up photo was on the atomic bomb dropped on Bikini Atoll?**

A. Rita Hayworth is certainly the bombshell in question. On July 1st 1946 one of the atomic bombs tested either had a picture of Rita Hayworth or the name 'Gilda' painted on it (after a character she played in a movie that cemented her popularity). In between 1946 and 1958 over 20 tests were conducted on Bikini Atoll, located in the Central Pacific.

Q. **Did they find Rasputin's body and how exactly did he die?**

A. Rasputin was served crème cakes and wine laced heavily with potassium cyanide, by Prince Felix Yusupov. When that failed to kill him he was shot three times and then drowned in the Neva River. The body of Rasputin was found 3 days after his death, frozen under ice in the Neva River. His penis is still on display in a Moscow Museum.

Q. When was Jesus really born?

A. That's a tricky one. Experts agree that Jesus was born sometime between 7 BC and 4 BC. The December 25th birthday was proclaimed between AD 314–360.

Q. What was stored in Pandora's box?

A. Zeus crammed into Pandora's box all the diseases, sorrows, vices, & crimes that afflict humanity. Opened by Pandora two times, the first time evil was released and the second time hope.

Q. What is the oldest family name recorded?

A. The oldest hereditary European surname is O'Clery, which dates back from around AD 9.

Q. **Are ginger people a descendent from Neanderthal man?**

A. Scientists believe that the prevalence of the ginger gene in many of today's population provides evidence that early Homo sapiens bred with Neanderthals. This is because the gene is known to exist 100,000 years ago and therefore pre-dates Homo sapiens.

———

Q. **What are the Seven Wonders of the World?**

A. The 7 Wonders of the Modern world are: Empire State Building, Itaipu Dam, CN Tower, Panama Canal, Channel Tunnel, North Sea Protection Works, and Golden Gate Bridge. The 7 Wonders of the Ancient world are: Great Pyramids of Giza, The Hanging Gardens of Babylon, The Temple of Artemis, The Statue of Zeus at Olympia, The Mausoleum of Halicarnassus, The Colossus of Rhodes, The Pharos (temple) of Alexandria. The 7 Wonders of the Natural World are: Mount Everest, Great Barrier Reef, Grand Canyon, Victoria Falls, Harbour of Rio de Janeiro, Paricutin Volcano, Northern Lights (Aurora Borealis).

Q. In which year did McVities produce the 1st chocolate digestive?

A. McVities first chocolate digestive was produced in 1925.

Q. Which Welsh legend was killed by the English, in 1282?

A. That would be Prince Llywelyn. He was separated from his army in December 1282 and killed by an English knight unaware of the Welsh prince's identity.

Q. Who was the longest reigning monarch in the world?

A. The longest reigning monarch in modern history is King Bhumibol Adulyadej, the 9th monarch of the Charkri Dynasty. He began his reign on June 9th 1946. He currently resides in Thailand.

Q. **Where were the first Olympics held?**

A. The first modern Olympics were held in
1896 in Athens, Greece. This was a return
after 1,503 years; ancient Olympics ran from
AD 776 to AD 393, in Olympia, Greece.

Q. **How long did the 100 Years War last?**

A. The 100 Years War was from 1337–1565 –
actually about 228 years. Most journals
suggest that the 100 Years War lasted until
1453 (116 years) because the only part of
France the English controlled after that date
was Calais.

Q. **How long did the Great Wall of China
take to build?**

A. The Wall construction began in 208 BC and
was finished in around AD 1620.
Construction lasted over 1,800 years.

Q. What island off Iceland in 1963 erupted?

A. In November 1963, a volcano exploded off the coast of Iceland, creating the island of Surtsey.

Q. What year was beer first put into cans?

A. Krueger's Finest Beer and Krueger's Cream Ale were the first beers to be sold in cans. This was in January 1935. Richmond, Virginia, USA.

Q. Where is Atlantis?

A. No one knows for sure where Atlantis was. A few ideas: Atlantis is the Azores, a Greek island, South China seas or just simply a story invented by Plato.

Q. Who is the greatest King/Conqueror of all time?

A. Alexander the Great is considered (by some) the greatest conqueror of all time. Remarkably, he had conquered 90 per cent of the known world by the age of 25.

Q. What is 'Trial by Ordeal' in Anglo–Saxon England?

A. In Anglo–Saxon England, the 'Trial by Ordeal' meant the accused had to perform a test (for example putting one's hand through flames) to determine guilt.

Q. How did the Crips gang come about?

A. The Crips were formed by Stan 'Tookie' Williams and Raymond Washington in LA in 1969 after the demise of the power of the Black Panthers and a need to control violence in their communities.

Q.   Was Santa Claus as we know him today
     (red costume) created by Coca-Cola or is
     that just an urban myth?

A.   Until the 1930s Santa Claus, Father
     Christmas, St Nicholas was presented in
     many fashions. In 1931 Coke ads by Swedish
     artist Haddon Sundblom depicted Santa in
     Coca-Cola colours; the idea stuck.

Q.   Who invented stage diving at gigs?

A.   Iggy Pop is one of the first musicians to have
     stage dived. Initially seen as confrontational
     and extreme, stage diving has become
     common.

Q.   'Nike' is the goddess of what?

A.   In Greek mythology, Nike was a goddess
     who personified triumph & victory.

Q.   What do Toltecs believe in?

A.   The Toltecs, were a Central American-living people between AD 900–1200, who allegedly followed the cult of Quetzalcoatl, the plumed serpent, known to demand human hearts as sacrifice.

———

Q.   Who was the most corrupt pope?

A.   There are several candidates, but Pope Alexander VI (Rodrigo Borgia), reputed to be a murderer, pimp and pornographer, wins our vote!

———

Q.   What was the name and circumstances of death of the Tory MP who died in an auto-erotic asphyxiation accident involving fruit and what was his constituency?

A.   On February 7th 1994, Eastleigh MP Stephen Milligan was found dead, tied to a chair with a plastic bag over his head and a Satsuma stuffed into his mouth.

Q.   Who was the secretary sacked for saying that 9/11 was a good day for burying bad news?

A.   Stephen Byers' (the Transport, Local Government and Region Secretary) press advisor, Jo Moore, was sacked from office for this statement.

———

Q.   How many United States presidents have been assassinated?

A.   There are four US Presidents who were assassinated: Abraham Lincoln, James Garfield, William McKinley and John F. Kennedy.

———

Q.   What was the name of Richard Nixon's dog?

A.   Richard M. Nixon, 37th President of the United States, had a dog named Checkers.

Q.   **What is Che Guevara's real first name?**

A.   Che Guevara's full name was Dr. Ernesto Guevara de la Serna (June 14th 1928 to October 9th 1967).

Q.   **What date did Victor Yushchenko the Ukrainian politician get poisoned?**

A.   The date of actual poisoning unknown; however, by December 2004 doctors confirmed Yushchenko was poisoned with TCDD dioxin.

Q.   **What implement was Trotsky murdered with?**

A.   Trotsky was attacked in his home in Mexico by Stalinist agent Ramon Mercader, who drove an ice pick into his skull.

Q. What was the MC5's political party called?

A. The White Panthers were a political
    collective founded in Detroit in 1968 by
    John Sinclair and proto-punk band MC5.

———

Q. Who tried to assassinate President Ronald
    Reagan?

A. On March 30th 1981, John Hinckley, 26,
    shot Ronald Reagan in attempt to attract
    attention of young actress Jodie Foster.

———

Q. Who was the only British prime minister
    to be assassinated?

A. Spencer Perceval (Tory PM 1809–1812) is
    the only PM to be murdered in office, shot
    dead in lobby of the House of Commons by
    merchant John Bellingham.

Q. **Which politician did Clement Freud describe as 'Attila the Hen'?**

A. 'Attila the Hen' was Clement Freud's nickname for Margaret Thatcher.

Q. **What is President George W. Bush's IQ?**

A. Since 1973, Lovenstein Institute has published IQ of each president. Bush's IQ is 91 but this result was affected by his dyslexia so it's not necessarily an accurate reflection.

Q. **Which British prime minister's father was a trapeze artist?**

A. John Major's family had a travelling variety troupe who toured the UK. At one time the PM performed as a trapeze artist called 'Tom Major'.

Q. **Who will win the next US Presidential election?**

A. According to odds checker, Hillary Clinton is currently 11/4 favourite to become the next American president.

Q. **Who is Idi Amin?**

A. Idi Amin was the President of Uganda (1971–1979) whose regime was notorious for its brutality. According to sources, 300,000 to 500,000 Ugandans were murdered during his rule.